The Tibetan Vinaya: A Guide to Buddhist Conduct

by

Bibliotheca Indo-Buddhica Series No. - 188

The Tibetan Vinaya: A Guide to Buddhist Conduct

by

The Venerable Khenchen
Thrangu Rinpoche
Geshe Rabjam
and
Abbot of Rumtek Monastery

Translated by
Sonam Palden
and
Chojor Radha

Sri Satguru Publications
A Division of
Indian Books Centre
Delhi, India

Published by :
Sri Satguru Publications
A Division of :
Indian Books Centre
Indological and Oriental Publishers
40/5, Shakti Nagar,
Delhi-110007
(INDIA)

ISBN 81-7030-571-3

First Edition : Delhi, 1998

Acknowledgements

We would like to thank the many persons who helped make this book possible. We would especially like to thank the staff of the *Profound Path of Peace* who first transcribed, edited, and published this teaching.

Note:

Techinal terms are italicized the first time that they are used to alert the reader that they may be found in the Glossary of Terms.

The Sanskrit letter c is pronounced "ch" and the Sanskrit letter ś and ṣ is pronounced "sh" and the Sanskrit ṛ is pronounced "ri" so we have added these letters to make pronunciation easier. Their actual spelling can be found in the Glossary of Terms.

Tibetan words are given as they are pronounced, not spelled in Tibetan. For their actual spelling see the Glossary of Tibetan Terms.

We use the convention of B.C.E. (Before Current Era) for the dates B.C. and and C.E. (Current Era) for A.D.

Published by Sunil Gupta for Sri Satguru Publications a division of Indian Books Centre, 40/5, Shakti Nagar, Delhi - 110 007, India and printed at Mudran Bharti, Delhi - 110 009

Contents

Foreword

Traditionally, the Buddhist teachings are divided into three major divisions called the Tripiṭaka. The Tripiṭaka consists of the Sūtras, the Vinaya, and the Abhidharma. The Sutras are the actual discourses of the Buddha, the Vinaya are the discourses of the Buddha on the conduct of the monks and nuns and also lay persons, and the Abhidharma is a complex classification of Buddhist concepts.

Reading through the discourses of the Buddha, one discovers that he was followed by thousands and thousands of monks and some nuns. These ordained individuals wanted to engage in the task of reaching enlightenment without being encumbered by family or worrying about livelihood. The Buddha taught these individuals a set of rules which became the Vinaya so that they could devote their complete energy to reaching enlightenment. The Buddha, however, did not simply one day say that these are the rules for ordained persons. Rather he waited for the proper situation to arise and would give a teaching on that situation. For example, one day some of his students reported that his monks, who were not allowed to have very many possessions, were taking their begging bowls and making these out of precious woods and embroidering them with precious jewels. The Buddha then gave a short teaching in which he said that monks should not embellish their begging bowls. This went on throughout the Buddha's lifetime and after the Buddha passed away, all these rules for the saṅgha were collected together and these were systematize into over 200 rules which came to be known as the Vinaya.

Since this time, the world has changed and there have been occasional calls for changing these rules of the Vinaya.

For example, in Buddha's day all ordinary persons slept on straw mats on the floor and only kings and wealthy merchants slept on beds. So one of the rules of the Vinaya is that monks and nuns could not sleep in a high bed. Clearly, today when almost everyone sleeps in a bed, this prohibition seems antiquated. Yet, when there has been a call to modernize the Vinaya, the Buddhist have almost always chosen to remain with the original rules of the Vinaya and to interpret these rules in a modified fashion. This interpretation of the rules is not just a practice of convenience, because deciding what is proper and what is improper is always made by highly evolved individuals who follow the criteria carefully laid out by the Buddha for deciding whether an act results in positive or negative karma.

To determine whether an action will produce negative karma it has to meet the four-fold criteria of basis, motivation, action, and final result. For example, for something to create negative karma that comes from stealing (a) the basis is that what is taken belongs to another, (b) the motivation is that one wants to deliberately take it, (c) the actions is that one actually takes it, and (d) the final result is that it is actually taken.

The author of this teaching, Thrangu Rinpoche, is eminently qualified for explaining the Vinaya and Buddhist conduct because he has lived since the age of four in a monastic situation. More recently he had spent seventeen years at Rumtek monastery in Sikkim at his Holiness Karmapa's monastery teaching the major Tulkus of the Kagyu Lineage of Tibetan Buddhism. Thrangu Rinpoche has maintained the his vows and was asked by Trungpa Rinpoche to become abbot of Gampo Abbey which is one of the few Tibetan monasteries in North America.

In August 1985 Thrangu Rinpoche visited Gampo Abbey for the first time and gave a seminar on monastic discipline. Rinpoche gave the first set of talks to a group of twenty people assembled with Sonam Palden translating.

These eight talks were on the prātimokṣha precepts. These were edited by Thelma Habgood published in Number 5 and 6 of *The Profound Path of Peace* which is the official journal of the International Kagyu Sangha Association

Thrangu Rinpoche then gave another series of talks to Gampo Abbey in 1988 and these talks were on the Three Vows. We have combined these talks into one book. The second set of teachings was a set of five talks given at Gampo Abbey in May of 1988 on the three vows and translated by Chojor Radha.

We would like to thank *The Profound Path of Peace* for publishing these talks and felt that for them to reach a wider audience, Namo Buddha Publications would combine the talks into a single volume.

Anyone interested in subscribing in *The Profound Path of Peace* which will continue to publish talks by Thrangu Rinpoche and other great lamas can write to The Profound Path of Peace, Gampo Abbey, Pleasant Bay, Nova Scotia, Canada BOE 2PO.

Clark Johnson, Ph. D.

Anyone wanting to know more about the activities or the programs or publications of Thrangu Rinpoche should contact the Namo Buddha Seminar, 1390 Kalmia Avenue, Boulder, CO 80304-1813. Phone: (303) 449-6608.

Table 1

The Five Precepts observed by lay devotees

1. Abstaining from destroying life

2. Abstaining from taking what is not given

3. Abstaining from sexual misconduct

4. Abstaining from false speech

5. Abstaining from anything that causes intoxication or mindlessness

Chapter 1

The Prātimokṣha Precepts

Buddha gave three main sets of teachings. The first teachings were the teachings on the *four noble truths* which were given at Sarnath, India and became the foundation for the *Theravādin* school. The second set of teachings were the teachings on *emptiness* and these were given at Rājagṛiha and became the foundation of the *mahāyāna* school of Buddhism. The third set of teachings were the *vajrayāna* teachings and were given in many different places. The *prātimokṣha precepts*[1] are currently practiced in Burma, Sri Lanka, and Thailand. In Korea and China which predominantly practice the mahāyāna teachings, the prātimokṣha are also practiced but with an emphasis on the bodhichitta precepts. In Tibet all three levels of precepts are practiced: the prātimokṣha, *bodhichitta*, and vajrayāna precepts.

Outwardly, the rules for Tibetan monks and nuns appear to be fairly relaxed. Theravādin and mahāyāna monks sometimes think that Tibetan monks are so lax that they do not observe the precepts. This is not true. In India, the monks can go begging for alms in the morning and come back in the

[1]There are actually eight levels of the prātimokṣa vows. First fully ordained monks take the bhikṣu (Tib. gelong) and nuns the bhikṣunī (Tib. gelongma) vows which number several hundred. Then there are vows for novice monks (Skt. śhrāmaṇera) and novice nuns (Skt. śhrāmaṇerikā) and training nuns (Skt. śhikśāmaṇa). Then there are five vows which can be taken by laymen (Skt. upāsaka) and laywomen (Skt. upāsikā). Finally, anyone may take the precepts on special lunar days (Skt. upāvasatha).

afternoon. But Tibet has no large cities and the Tibetan villages are spread far and wide. So even if the monks went out begging for alms at four o'clock in the morning, they would not be able to return until late in the evening and would therefore be unable to practice and study. Therefore, the Tibetan *paṇḍitas* and *siddhas* in the past decided that rather than spending the whole day begging for alms, it would be preferable for monks and nuns to spend the time on practice and study. So Tibetan monks do not go out begging for alms.

Tibetan monks also eat in the afternoon which, in the view of some people, is breaking the precepts.[2] But there is a reason for this. In India, the monks go begging alms in the morning and come back in the afternoon and do their meditation in the evening. It is not proper to beg for alms both in the morning and the evening. Since the monks depend on alms for food, the Buddha forbid the nuns and monks to eat in the evening. However, in Tibet the monks do not go for alms and so can eat in the afternoon or evening if they are still hungry to allow them to better study and practice.

Tibetan monks also eat meat whereas Chinese monks do not. But again the Theravādin monks do this because when they beg alms and have to take whatever food they get from the patron, whether it is meat or fish or vegetables. Because the monk may receive meat while begging, the Buddha in the *Vinaya sūtra* did not prohibit the eating of meat. Chinese monks do not eat meat but they eat sea food. They do not eat meat because by not eating meat the hundreds of worms that may be in the meat are saved. Similarly, in Tibet the meat that comes only from large animals is eaten. So, for example, the meat of one yak is sufficient for one monk for one year. Also, by eating vegetarian food, one might kill more living beings than one yak in the process of cultivating the various

[2]In the sūtras the Buddha specifically states that monks and nuns should not eat any solid food after noontime.

vegetable crops. Therefore the Tibetan paṇḍitas and siddhas decided that it was better to eat one yak than to kill many small animals thus maintaining the precepts in an appropriate way. By eating only large animals not only are the prātimokṣha precepts, but also the bodhichitta precepts[3] and the vajrayāna precepts[4] are maintained. This, however, is not saying that Tibetan monks are perfect precept holders.

Tibetan monks wear maroon robes while Theravādin monks wear yellow and Chinese monks wear black. The Buddha instructed ordained monks to wear red, yellow, or blue robes with the color maroon not being authorized by the Buddha. Therefore the mahāyāna and Theravādin Buddhist monks do not use maroon robes. However, the Tibetan paṇḍitas and siddhas rejected the color blue because this is a color worn by lay people and chose maroon instead.[5]

At the time of the Buddha, the monks in India did not wear the vest that Tibetan monks wear and kept the upper part of their body naked. When Indian paṇḍitas came to Tibet, they found it was so cold that they had to wear the seat-cover (Tib. *ding ba*) all the time. So the vest was copied from that and later on changes were made in the design to symbolize the six *pāramitās*. This then became the uniform of the Tibetan monk.

Now we are in America, and ordained monks and nuns are flourishing. I believe that in a modern society it is not

[3] The bodhisattva precepts (explained in great detail later) is the vow to help all sentient beings obtain enlightenment.
[4]The vajrayāna precepts also explained in greater detail later are to maintain all one's commitments and practices.
[5]According to Khenpo Karthar the maroon dye was almost unavailable in India and therefore too expensive to be considered for monk's robes. Also according to Khenpo Karthar maroon dye was abundant in Tibet and therefore inexpensive and easily accessible.

appropriate to go out begging alms, but it is more appropriate to eat in accordance with the customs of the Tibetan monks, like eating food in the evening. However, during the time of the bimonthly purification practice (Tib. *sojong*) and during the rainy season retreats (Tib. *yarne*), it would be fitting to not eat in the evenings in memory of the Buddha's instructions. I also believe that one should stop eating the meat of small animals and eat the meat of only large animals.

Questions

Question: Rinpoche, in the West we have the idea that an animal like a dog or cow is higher than a worm or an ant.
Rinpoche: In the Buddhist tradition, everything that has life has feeling. So it doesn't make any difference whether it is small or big. The killing of a human being, however, is regarded as a particularly bad negative action, because human beings can achieve a higher goal and be helpful to other beings. But there is no difference between dog, worm, or cow.
Question: One of the contradictions that we run into with our nonBuddhist friends is that they say that we don't kill but we eat meat. We say yes, but it is third hand. But that doesn't help them understand. Can you say something about meat that has to passed through three hands?
Rinpoche: The Buddha said that meat can be eaten if one is free from the threefold conceptualization, that (a) one does not kill animals directly for oneself, (b) one does not persuade others to kill animals for oneself to eat, and (c) that the animals are not actually killed by another person in order to feed oneself. If one is free from these three conceptualizations, then the meat can be eaten.
Question: In this area there are a lot of local fishermen who fish for a livelihood and brought us fish, both because we asked them for it and as a gift. I wonder how we should relate to this situation.

Rinpoche: You should stop saying, "Please bring fish for us." But if they bring fish and offer it to you, then that is not bad.
Question: Should we buy it from them off the dock?
Rinpoche: Yes, then you are buying a dead fish. When the fish is already dead, whether you buy it or they offer it to you it is the same.
Question: If everyone stopped buying fish, they wouldn't kill them.
Rinpoche: Even if we Buddhists would stop eating fish, there are a lot of other people who would eat fish.
Question: But what about the precept not to kill?
Rinpoche: Eating meat and keeping the precept of not killing are totally different since we are not killing the fish ourselves, we are buying it from someone else. If we refrain from killing animals for food, that is an act that is beneficial to the animal. However, if there is an animal already slaughtered, refraining from eating it does not help the dead animal and the meat will rot.
Question: But it always comes to the idea that the animal will be killed. In fact, the negative action or is left to others so you will stay pure. If you are a good *bodhisattva*, you should take it on yourself instead of leaving it to others.
Rinpoche: We have to undergo our own individual *karma*. What is most important is preventing negative actions done by ourself. It would be very good if we could persuade others not to do negative actions. But mostly it depends on the individual. For instance, I once made a similar mistake. I found a cobweb in the bathroom and thought that the spider was going to kill many other insects. So I broke the spider web with my fingers and prevented the spider from getting food for itself. Actually my intention was to protect the small insects the spider might kill and eat, but instead the spider itself was harmed because it was not able to get food and died from hunger.

Question: Chogyam Trungpa Rinpoche suggested that we try to be mainly vegetarian at Gampo Abbey which means that we need to have a garden. So we had to kill insects if we were going to have carrots and onions and potatoes.
Rinpoche: What is most important is motivation. Since we have the motivation not to kill any sentient beings, even if we dig in the ground to grow the vegetables, that's not very bad. What is important according to the *Vinaya* is not to have the intention to kill.
Question: If there are a thousand Buddhists in Boulder, Colorado and each one of them eats one chicken each week: that's 52,000 chickens in a year. And since everything is computerized, the producers know that they will raise these extra 52,000 chickens because they know they will be eaten. If the Buddhists didn't eat chicken, they wouldn't raise them.
Rinpoche: If one buys say eight hundred fish at the market today, tomorrow they are replaced by eight hundred new fish. Any action is their karma, not one's own. But from one's own point of view there may be the foundation, but there is no intention or motivation. Thus one may have the intention of eating meat, but one does not have the intention of killing the animal. Since not all of the four factors are present, it is not a violation of the precept.
Question: What about the active intention of trying to stop others from killing? If one thousand Buddhists stopped eating chicken, they would actually have the chance of stopping the chicken breeders from killing. They wouldn't be able to make money, so they won't kill them.
Rinpoche: In this realm we cannot persuade others not to kill. For example, in the oceans how many small fish are killed by the bigger fish? What is important is for us to refrain from killing, and in that way we can stop killing. It is not possible to persuade others.
Question: At Gampo Abbey we take the five precepts daily. Should we formally take this precept of not killing knowing

that later in the day we are going to stick a shovel through many worms or whatever. Does it make a difference if our motivation is to develop food here? Does it make a difference whether that precept for that day is formally taken or not?

Rinpoche: It's appropriate to take the precept even though we may kill insects while working. Since we have the motivation not to kill them, then we are not killing intentionally.

Question: Very often we have to make a decision about what situation is a greater benefit. In modern society people often decide to kill some animals in order to provide bigger benefit, for instance, the control of malaria which is spread by mosquitoes. The only way to control malaria is to kill the mosquitoes.

Rinpoche: I think that if one has a pure motivation for the benefit of others then it's not bad to kill insects. If one has the desire for fame or money and kills mosquitoes with that sort of intention, then, of course, that's bad.

Table 2

The 10 virtuous deeds promulgated by King Songtsen Gampo of Tibet

Three virtuous deeds of the body:

1. Refraining from killing
2. Refraining from stealing
3. Refraining from sexual misconduct

Four virtuous deeds of speech

1. Refraining from lying
2. Refraining from slander
3. Refraining from harsh words
4. Refraining from senseless or idle talk

Three virtuous deeds of mind

1. Refraining from covetousness
2. Refraining from ill will
3. Refraining from wrong views.

Chapter 2

Discipline and the Precepts

During the reign of the first Tibetan dharma king Songtsen Gampo (617-698 C. E.), the practice of the Buddhist teachings were introduced to lay people and then about four generations later the practice of the ordained monastics was established. However, in America the practice of lay people and of monastics were established at the same time (in the 1970s) within one generation. In Tibet lay practitioners wore long hair and white clothes and the ordained monks wore maroon and yellow robes. Later during the reign of king Langdarma (ruled 901-906 C. E.), the teachings of the Buddha were suppressed by eliminating all ordained persons, but the lay practitioners were able to preserve the teachings. That is why lay practitioners are regarded as very important in the Tibetan tradition.

Taking full ordination provides the monk or nun with more opportunity to practice and study which helps them to lead a peaceful and smooth life. This *discipline* is (Skt. *śhīla*, Tib. *tsultrim*), literally meaning "cool." Being cool was particularly important in India because it is such a hot country. The Buddha compared the life of lay people to a pit of fire, because their minds were constantly tormented by all sorts of worldly problems and they were constantly engaged in busy activities. On the other hand, the life of monks and nuns was like living in a cool house, because they had no worldly concerns such as children, spouses, or worldly possessions to worry about. The life of lay people may appear to be more enjoyable because they can sing and dance and so on, but in fact monastic life is much more peaceful and harmonious. The pleasures and enjoyment of lay life have no essence and are rooted in suffering. That is why, after being ordained, there is more opportunity and leisure to practice and meditate properly. After taking the vows, one might feel imprisoned because one cannot do this or that, but actually, as one abandons what needs to be abandoned, one finds one is more relaxed in a more simple and smooth state.

There are four main precepts that monks and nuns take. The first precept is not to steal. We may think that by taking something without the owner's knowledge we can have it without spending any money. We may be successful the first time we steal and not be discovered or we may be caught stealing. If we are successful, our mind will not be content and we will wish for more and more and fall into a habitual pattern of stealing. If, however, we make the commitment in front of our teacher or a statue of the Buddha, not to steal from this time onward, we need not be afraid of anybody else. Our problem is solved and we feel we have much more freedom.

The second precept is refraining from sexual intercourse. A boy driving with his girl friend in a nice car may seem to be having a very enjoyable time, but inwardly he may be constantly worried that he might do something that would hurt the girl, that she might get sick, or that he might do something to make her unhappy. So if they have a good relationship it causes problems; if they don't have a good relationship, then it causes problems of another sort. But if one takes the vow not to have sexual intercourse, then from that time on one is free from this kind of suffering of constantly worrying about one's sexual relationships.

The third precept is not killing sentient beings. If one has not taken the vow, one might try to solve one's problems by killing one's enemy and running away. But the relatives and the friends of the enemy will now also become one's enemies adding to the problem. Also, one may not take the vow of not killing simply because one believes that the situation will never occur. But some day that situation might arise. Therefore, if one takes the vow not to kill, one is completely free from the suffering caused by these problems.

The fourth precept is to refrain from telling lies. One might think that one can escape from problems by telling lies, but this is not the case. The Sākya Paṇḍita has said that by lying, one may have the intention of deceiving others, but in fact, one is deceiving oneself. If one tells a lie once, afterwards people will not believe one even if one is telling the truth. If one tells a lie to one's enemy or to someone in whom one has no confidence, then that person will not believe one anyway. If one tells a lie to someone with whom one has a good relationship, then from that time onward they will lose confidence in one and the relationship will be spoiled. So by starting to tell lies one will become like an echo and nobody will believe you.

The Four Factors

In accordance with the Buddha's teachings, if one follows the precepts of not stealing, not killing, not having sexual intercourse, and not lying, then one's life becomes harmonious and "cool" with this discipline.

With each of these four precepts there must be four factors or conditions met before the precept is actually broken. These are: foundation, motivation, action, and final results. If we take the precept of not stealing, the "foundation" is something that belongs to another person that is useful to him. If one takes something worthless like a needle and thread from someone, that is not very negative. The second factor is "motivation." If one has impure motivation and knows that these things belong to another and wants to steal them, then that constitutes stealing. If, however, one does not have the motivation to steal, such as taking another's belongings by mistake or taking them from a friend knowing that the friend would have no objection, then that is not a negative action. The third factor is "action." Merely having the intention of stealing itself is not sinful. But following up the intention with the act of stealing is a definite negative action. The fourth factor is the "final result." If, for example, one has the intention of stealing another's belonging and one becomes so ill that one can not actually take the possession, then that is not a negative action leading to negative karma.

For those who are ordained and have taken the vows, the foundation for the precept of not killing is the human being. However, for those who are not fully ordained but who have taken the precepts, the foundation is whatever has a mind (Tib. *sem*). The second factor of motivation, is very important while cultivating crops, one may unintentionally kill many insects and worms. Or one may throw a stone from the top of a hill which accidentally may kill some animal. The third factor is "action." Even if one has the intention to kill a human being or a sentient being as long as the action is not executed, the precept is not broken. The fourth factor is "final result." Even if one has the motivation to kill someone and one goes through the action of killing, but the human being doesn't die, then there is no sin of killing.

The Buddha himself said that all four factors must be present together to constitute a sin. So if the four factors are present while relating to a particular precept, then that precept is broken, but if the four factors are not present together, then the precept is unbroken.

Questions

Question: You said that the foundation for killing is having a mind. Would you explain sentient beings or higher forms further?

Rinpoche: If you cut or destroy flowers, plants and vegetables, they will die because they have life, but they don't have feelings or a mind. So mind refers to animals, insects, worms, or whatever has feelings. Scientifically, people may distinguish various shades of animate and inanimate, but I myself distinguished animate and inanimate in accordance with the teachings of the Buddha.

Question: Rinpoche, perhaps I misunderstood what you said when you were talking about the foundation. You differentiated between the foundation whether one was a fully ordained person or whether one had just taken layman's precepts. I would have assumed that the foundation for the fully ordained person would be a more restricted situation, but it seems the other way around.

Rinpoche: That was not a misunderstanding, those who are fully ordained have taken the vow not to kill a human being. If they kill insects or small animals, that is a sin, of course, but it is not a violation of the *parajika* vow of fully ordained monastics. But in the case of those who have taken the lay precepts, for example, *upāsakas,* since they have taken the vow not to kill any sentient being, if they kill an insect or small animal, then that is a violation of their vow. When I say fully ordained I am talking about *gelong* ordination. Novice and fully ordained have the same vow.

Question: Rinpoche, in our *saṅgha,* drinking and sexual relationships are very widespread, which leads sometimes to chaos because people don't know how to handle those things properly. If one took the precepts as a lay practitioner, one might be the only person in a particular saṅgha to do that and that might be very difficult to maintain.

Rinpoche: If one takes the precepts, that's very good; but even if one does not take the precepts, one can still practice them. This is a matter of motivation. In the *Jataka Tales* the stories of the previous lives of the Buddha, there is a story when the Buddha was the captain of a ship with five hundred sailors. His name at that time was "Great Courage." There was a very evil man whose intention was to kill all the five hundred passengers on the ship by making a hole in the ship. Great Courage saw that this man was about to make the hole in the ship and thought it would be a great sin for him to kill five hundred people. He thought, "If I kill this evil man, it will save the lives of five hundred people and also stop the evil man from falling into hell." So Great Courage killed him by hitting him in the head with an ax. So killing the evil-minded man was not a sin for Great Courage, rather it was a virtuous act. That is why motivation is so important. Coming back to the question of alcohol and sexual intercourse which you say is contradictory to *dharma* practice. Based on these actions, many people will grow in intention and attitude towards dharma practice. I think that intoxicants and sexual intercourse are not bad for lay people. However, for monks and nuns who have taken vows, that's another matter.

Question: Rinpoche, in western culture there is the notion of a "white lie" that is, sometimes you lie out of kindness for people. For example, you might tell your mother something that wasn't completely true because you don't want to hurt her.

Rinpoche: A white lie isn't bad since one is telling it with a good motivation.

Chapter 3

The Vow of Individual Liberation

The Tibetan word for "individual liberation" is *so sor tharpa dompa* or prātimokṣha in Sanskrit. The word prātimokṣha is quite similar to the word for discipline (Skt. *śhīla*) which we have already discussed. Temporary liberation means liberation from the sufferings and problems of day-to-day life. Ultimate liberation means being ultimately free from the suffering of *saṃsāra.* The Tibetan word *so sor* or *prāti* in Sanskrit means "individual" or "personal." For example, if we follow the precept of not killing and don't kill, then we are personally free from any negative results that come from killing. If we have taken the vow not to steal and don't steal, then we are free from the causes of suffering that comes from stealing. Thus, by following all the precepts, we will be free from all suffering. The nature of prātimokṣha vows is basically refraining from harming others either directly or indirectly. Direct causes of harm are, for example, killing or stealing. An example of indirect cause of harm is singing and dancing, which does not have direct harmful results, but gradually results in harm. So the essence of prātimokṣha is to abandon the primary cause of harming others directly as well as the secondary cause which may harm indirectly.

When we take the prātimokṣha vows, our motivation may be impure and this attitude should be abandoned. There are two types of impure motivation. First we may have expectations of temporary happiness resulting from ordination or we have the desire to protect ourselves from temporary unfavorable condition such as an illness. Second, we may expect to receive respect and veneration from others or hope to be free from rules and regulations by taking ordination.

There are also two types of motivation. The first which is not the motivation at the time of taking the prātimokṣha vows, is the cultivation of bodhichitta for the benefit of all sentient beings. The second is the wish to eliminate all suffering in this lifetime as well as all future lifetimes. Discipline is like a *wish-fulfilling jewel.* If we look upon discipline as a cause of temporary comfort, then the prātimokṣha vows will bring about temporary relief from suffering. If we abandon the thought of temporary comfort and look upon the prātimokṣha vows as the cause for eliminating suffering, ultimately then it will be the cause of freeing oneself ultimately from saṃsāra.

When we take the prātimokṣha vow we are following the example of the *arhats* of the past and we proclaim that we will follow their path in the same way. First we have the motivation, then we takes the vow, and finally we must keep the precepts. We proclaim:

> Just as the arhats of the past followed and preserved the precepts of not killing, not stealing, not committing sexual intercourse, not lying, not becoming intoxicated, etc. so also will I follow and preserve the precepts.
>
> In the past the arhats abandoned the thought of harming others and abandoned the cause of harming others. Having abandoned whatever has to be abandoned and having realized whatever has to be realized, they eventually attained the realization of arhat. So too will I do the same and follow the training that the arhats underwent.

At the time of taking the prātimokṣha vow one should have the yellow robe (Tib. *chogo*), the begging bowl, and a strainer. The purpose of having these three is the intention of not harming others. Water which is used for drinking or washing should be stained through the strainer so as not to harm the small animals or insects that may be present in the water.

In order to protect one's vows, one should constantly have mindfulness and awareness and one must constantly think of abandoning what has to be abandoned. If certain parts of the vows are transgressed, the transgression should not be left alone but should be repaired. The Buddha said that one should have a high regard for one's discipline, one should cherish one's discipline. Cherishing one's discipline means having continuous mindfulness and awareness and repairing the vows immediately if they are broken. The Buddha said that to preserve the purity of the vows, one should have at least one of these two factors. If one has either of the two, then one can develop one's discipline and realize what has to be realized and attain the state of an arhat. If one has neither of these, one cannot develop one's discipline and cannot attain the ultimate goal.

The transmission of the prātimokṣha in Tibet is derived from the Mūlasarvāstivādin tradition. According to this Mūlasarvāstivādin, the vows of the fully ordained monastic, of the novice and of the layman are of two forms; that which can be perceived and that which cannot be perceived. At the time when the vow is actually taken, it is in the form which can be perceived because others can actually see one taking the vow. From then on, it becomes the form which cannot be perceived, because others cannot see that one has, for example, abandoned the action of killing. The actions of not killing, not stealing, and not engaging in sexual intercourse are virtuous actions of the body while not lying is the virtuous action of speech. One can preserve the vows directly or consciously, or indirectly such as at the time of eating or sleeping, since one already has the vows within oneself.

Questions

Question: You talked about preserving discipline with mindfulness and heedfulness and secondly if one violated one's vows, one should repair them. But it seems to me that it requires mindfulness and heedfulness to notice that one has violated one's vows.

Rinpoche: Since the prātimokṣha is the vow with perceived form, the violation will manifest itself. For instance, one may tell a lie during a time of not having mindfulness and heedfulness, but then later, when one recollects, one thinks "Oh, I told a lie."

Question: How would one make it up when the vow is broken?

Rinpoche: One makes it up by offering personal confession and during the bimonthly sojong confession ceremony.

Question: The vow seems to constitute an accessory cause of liberation because, you cannot really be purified just by outward behavior, but have to be purified by meditating. It seems to me that the vow by itself could not liberate.

Rinpoche: You are right in saying that one should meditate; meditation is very important, of course. One cannot attain enlightenment just having discipline without meditation. However, a person endowed with perfect discipline who cherishes his discipline, will never remain idle; he or she will always be engaged in practice. So by perfect discipline, one obtains the power to meditate. That is why discipline is powerful.

Question: What is the difference between the prātimokṣha and the bodhisattva vows?

Rinpoche: Prātimokṣha vows are always stated in negative form, in other words, "I will refrain from killing, I will refrain from lying, etc." Because they are stated in that way, it is always very clear whether or not they have been kept because you did something you weren't supposed to do. In the mahāyāna vows, there is the vow to increase one's compassion which seems to be much more a matter of degree.

The discipline of the prātimokṣha is based on body and speech, so whatever mistakes we make can be perceived immediately. But the mahāyāna vows deal mainly with our mind and so we cannot easily tell whether our discipline is progressing or declining. The mahāyāna vow is compared to a golden vase which can be easily damaged or broken, but also easily repaired. However, the prātimokṣha vows are like a big clay vase which can be damaged easily, but once it is damaged it breaks completely.

Question: It seems that vows that just refrain from certain kinds of actions don't solve a lot because they don't show, for example, the essence of mind.

Rinpoche: By refraining from impure actions one is freed from all mental or psychological problems. This helps one to stay in a peaceful state so that one's meditation can develop.

Question: If I refrain from impure activities over a period of time, then gradually I will develop a better frame of mind so that I can practice more. But how can the vows help flash on the essence of mind? As an example, sexuality doesn't seem to be a problem, per se. It seems that the by-products of sexuality cause the problems. Just saying no sexuality doesn't change too much.

Rinpoche: When one is meditating on subtle heat (Tib. *tummo*) one is not violating the precepts since one is not committing sexual intercourse and one does not lose one's drops, sperm (Skt. *bindu*, Tib. *tig lee*). Is that clear?

Question: We are not practicing subtle heat.

Rinpoche: In the future you will practice it.

Question: Rinpoche, would you agree that the precepts would not work without practice, but that the practice would work without the precepts?

Rinpoche: Your question was would it work if practice is without precepts. The precepts are important to accumulate merit. But without meditation, through the precepts alone, one cannot attain enlightenment. By meditating and abandoning all negative emotions, one can attain enlightenment. In order to abandon negative emotions, one must preserve one's discipline.

Question: Would there be a natural tendency for body, speech, and mind to progress towards right action if there were no precepts?

Rinpoche: It is difficult to meditate without the precepts. But there are exceptions like the king Indrabhūti who had five hundred queens. He had given up attachment and sexual intercourse for king Indrabhūti was not the same as for ordinary beings.

Question: Is there a natural tendency with meditation practice for the mind to go towards what is good. The precepts help, of course, but could we say, "Well, now we won't bother taking precepts, we will become naturally good through sitting practice alone."

Rinpoche: If we can just give up all negative emotions through practicing alone without taking precepts, that's fine, whether whether they are the prātimokṣha, the bodhichitta, or the vajrayāna vows. What is important is eradication of all the impurities, all negative emotions. So it makes no difference whether one eradicates the impurities through the discipline of the precepts or through meditation. Eliminating the impurities is the ultimate attainment.

Chapter 4

Karma and the Accumulation of Merit

The last chapter was on the Mūlasarvāstivādin system and the vows that exist in the perceived and unperceived forms. In general, the vows have special virtue and the power of accumulation of merit and virtue (Tib. *sonam kyi tsog)* are based on one's commitment. There is a difference, for example, between simply not killing and not killing after having taken the vow of not killing. When we simply abandon the action of not killing, it will not result in the fruition of not killing. For example, if a dog at the moment is not killing anything, then that dog is not violating the vow of not killing, but it also is not accumulating the virtue of not killing because it has not taken the vow. The reason for this is that, at present, the cause for killing is not present so the dog is not killing anything. But later when the cause for killing turns up, the dog may then kill something. Likewise, if we have not taken the vow not to kill, then even if we do not kill, we will gain no merit. But if we have taken the vow, then when we do not kill, we are also gaining the virtue of not killing since we have the motivation of refraining from the act of killing. So, we obtain the virtue of not killing because of our strong motivation not to kill. The difference between a dog and a man who has taken the vow not to kill is that the man will accumulate virtue whereas the dog will not. For instance, if we take the vow at six in the morning, then at seven o'clock we will have accumulated the virtue of not killing for one hour, at eight o'clock, for two hours and so on. When we chant *mantras*, we accumulate virtue with each mantra that we chant. So once we have taken the vow, we then accumulate the virtue of the vow. When we take the vow of not killing, we are refraining from killing not just one man but are refraining from killing all sentient beings and so the accumulation of virtue grows. Since we have the strong motivation that is constantly growing, then the accumulation of virtues continues whether we are playing, eating, or sleeping. But if our motivation for not killing is somehow broken, then from that time on the virtues cease to accumulate.

How do we cultivate the virtues even when we are asleep? If a man who has not taken the vow of not killing awakens from sleep, then he might commit the crime of killing depending on whether conditions are favorable or unfavorable for killing. On the other hand, if a man who has taken the vow awakens from sleep, he has the strong motivation not to kill, so he will refrain from killing and accumulates the virtue for the period of time while he was sleeping. Thus, if we maintain the five precepts, we are accumulating the merit of these five each minute. If we preserve ten precepts each minute, we are accumulating the merit of ten precepts. After having taken the vows, we may not see how the virtues are increasing within ourselves, but nevertheless from the moment of taking the vow onwards, the merit of preserving the vow will develop. For this reason, the Buddha emphasized moral discipline.

The ultimate effect of the accumulation of merit is enlightenment. The Tibetan word for the Buddha is *sang gye*. The syllable *sang* means "awakened" from the sleep of ignorance and *gye* means "to open up" like a flower. So *sangye* means awakened from all the negativities, all the delusions. When we eradicate all the negativities, the good qualities will blossom forth. All sentient beings already have the essence of enlightenment within them, so they possess all the qualities which are ready to blossom. It is like the sky. When the sun is obscured by clouds, we cannot see the rays of the sun. Likewise, we have the qualities of the essence of enlightenment within us but they are obscured by the defilements and negativities. Just as when clouds clear away, we can see the sun's rays, so when the obscurations are cleared away, the qualities of Buddhahood will blossom forth. That is why it is important to clear away all the defilements.

The nature of the defilements is like salty water. If we drink salty water, we become more and more thirsty and this causes us to drink even more salty water. In the same way, if we carry out the action of the defilements, it leads us to want to act again and again in the same way and so the defilements increase. The Tibetan *paṇḍitas* and *siddhas* have compared this to a pig entering a garden. As soon as the pig comes into the garden, one should hit it on the nose with a stick so that it won't go into the garden again. But if it is already in the garden and has started to eat the vegetables, then it is not so easy to get the pig out of the garden. Likewise, one should try to stop the negativities and defilements when they first arise in the mind; just as we hit the pig on the nose when it first starts to enter the garden.

Since beginningless time we have become habituated to working with the defilements. We shouldn't try to stop the defilements but when they first arise in the mind we should not follow them with our body and our speech. If we do not follow the defilements, then gradually our mind will be rid of the defilements. When our defilements decrease, our meditation practice will automatically progress. In this way, all the benefits are accomplished.

According to some Western psychologists, if we suppress our thoughts then the mind will be damaged and so we should immediately do whatever comes to our mind. For example, when we feel aggressive, we should tear up a piece of paper and not wait for the aggression to build up in ourselves. Someone once told me that when he gets angry, it helps him to beat his pillow. Maybe that's true.

Maybe when a thought arises, we should just wait and see what happens to that thought. But that is not the way to preserve the vows. For instance, if a man puts sweets on the table and then says to his children: "Don't eat these sweets" his children will develop a strong desire to eat the sweets. But in our case, preserving the vows, is quite different. It is like a man putting poison on the table and telling people: "Don't eat that poison, otherwise you will die." No one has the motivation to eat the poison; rather they have the motivation to abandon the poison and will try to find a way to throw the poison away.

The Buddha taught that one should refrain from the negativities and defilements because following them will cause us suffering. That is why we refrain from negative actions and also accumulate the benefits of eliminating negative actions.

It is not true that without taking the vows we cannot attain higher state of mind. In fact, in the Kagyu tradition, Tilopa, Nāropa, Gampopa, and Milarepa did not take the vows, but yet by their great diligence and wisdom, they were able to control their defilements and that served the same purpose as taking the vows. Tilopa, Nāropa, Marpa, and Milarepa are the most perfect teachers and lineage holders of our tradition and were able to attain Buddhahood in one lifetime.

Questions

Question: Rinpoche, what does it mean to accumulate virtue?

Rinpoche: Accumulation of virtue is the karma of action of body, speech, and mind. Action has two aspects: virtuous and unvirtuous. So virtue consists of whatever virtuous karma is accumulated through the virtuous actions of body, speech, and mind. Conversely, unvirtuous karma is whatever karma is accumulated through unvirtuous actions of body, speech, and mind.

Question: In terms of karmic situations, by maintaining the precepts, are we just not creating further karma, or are we repairing old karma as well?

Rinpoche: In terms of preserving the precepts, when negative karma is abandoned, then good karma can increase and the result is virtue. Karma is like a job. Our mundane life is based on what kind of job we have. If we have a good job then we can have a good life more or less, and if we don't have a good job we may not have such a good life. So by practicing positive karma through our body, speech, and mind, we can attain Buddhahood.

Question: My understanding is that cutting through the chain of karma brings us to Buddhahood, not the accumulation of good or bad karma, since we are still in saṃsāra, accumulating good or bad karma.

Rinpoche: Here is a very old example for this. Long ago, in order to make fire, one had to rub two sticks together very vigorously and when the fire ignites and it burns up both sticks. At the time of accumulating good karma, bad karma is abandoned and good karma is developed. Slowly all the defilements are controlled. By this process, all negativities are gradually destroyed and karma stops automatically. During the time of practicing, we try to accomplish good karma and abandon bad karma. It's like the two sticks rubbing together.

Gradually we are able to destroy all the negativities and karma stops by itself.

Question: Would you say something about the ripening of karma and how the practitioner experiences that?

Rinpoche: Generally, the explanation of ripening of karma is very subjective and hard to understand. The idea can be understood only through clear wisdom. But if we try to examine it by way of examples, then it is quite easy to understand. For instance, I was born in Tibet and if I think, "Why was I born in Tibet and why wasn't I born in America?" I can't think about that. The fact is simply that because of my previous karma I had to be born in Tibet. I may think why was I born in the year 1931 and why did I not die before 1959 so I wouldn't have to endure the suffering of the Chinese invasion. I get the same answer: everything that happened was due to my own past karma. If I want to come to America, I need a visa. But if you wonder why you were born in America, who gave you the visa? Your karma gave you the visa.

Question: It sounds like it is the responsibility of the individual to shape his or her own karma. But I wonder about freedom of decision. Karmapa seems to be the knower of the three times and Padmasambhava made predictions about what's happening in the future. How can you predict the future if karma is based on freedom?

Rinpoche: Clairvoyance cannot be conceived in ordinary terms. For example, a man may predict that in the future somebody will come here to build a factory and start a business. At the time of making the prediction, he will not know whether that person will come in the future or not, whether he will have the idea of building the factory or not. Also, in Tibet, prophecies were made that, in the future, a certain person will come and will have to undergo certain kinds of suffering. That is his karma that he is to undergo, but that can be predicted.

Question: But doesn't that contradict freedom, the power of free decision, to decide in which direction you will go?

Rinpoche: That is not contradictory to make a decision for oneself because when a prediction is made that someone is going to do such and such in the future, freedom of decision has not been taken away. Instead, what is being said is that someone is going to do that in the future.

Question: Karma sounds sometimes as if it always comes from the past. But could it come from a vision of a desirable future. For example, if I see a vision to build Gampo Abbey, therefore it's part of my karma and part of my power is to be able to fulfill that vision. I'm trying to resolve karma and freedom in my mind. What's happening now to any one of us is simply the result of the past. Maybe it's the result of a vision of the future. You said that Padmasambhava made a prediction. Maybe that prediction is his vision of a desirable future and he sees it is possible that it could be that way, so he makes that prediction.

Rinpoche: When Padmasambhava came to Tibet in the eighth century, he predicted that in the future the iron bird would fly west and that the dharma would flourish in that country. At that time there were no airplanes, no iron birds, but now we have them. So there doesn't seem to be any contradiction in predicting the future even if it doesn't exist at the present time.

Question: Rinpoche emphasized the importance of taking the vow to do virtuous activity so that there would be an effective accumulation of merit. It seems to me there are two aspects to say not killing: realization that there is no need to be angry and also the understanding of how to respond in a compassionate way in the situation.

Rinpoche: For example, if we vow not to kill, we have the strong motivation not to kill then if thoughts of killing arises in our mind and our bodily action will not go along with the thought of killing. Then slowly we will become accustomed to the thought of refraining from killing, and thus the defilements of the mind will slowly be purified. Body and speech support the mind. If bodily actions always follow after the mind, then the mind becomes stronger and stronger. But if actions of body and speech stop, then the mind is no longer supported by body and speech and the mind grows weaker and weaker.

Question: It seems that there may be times when one has to do an unskillful action when there are enemies who are trying to destroy the dharma or harm the guru. How do you do that without violating your bodhisattva vow and your precepts?

Rinpoche: There are slight differences in intention among the three levels of vows. One should act from the level which is the most appropriate, the level with which one can relate most reasonably. These three levels of vows are interrelated. For instance at the prātimokṣha level, the hīnayāna level, it is said that one should "suppress" the defilements. In Tibetan this word "suppress" means one should not completely eliminate the defilements but that one should literally "press them on their heads" so that they cannot stand up. By so doing, that helps the meditation on the mahāyāna and vajrayāna levels.

Chapter 5

The Outer, Inner, and Secret Prātimokṣha

According to the *tantrayāna*, the prātimokṣha is classified as outer, inner, and secret, corresponding to the hīnayāna path, the mahāyāna path and the vajrayāna path respectively. But the purpose of all three prātimokṣha vows is to tame the mind and free oneself from delusion. There is, however, a difference in their approach. The hīnayāna prātimokṣha is called the path of abandonment. As we have said before, according to the Theravāda system, we should not allow delusions to arise and should not allow actions of body, speech, and mind go along with the delusions. Unvirtuous actions of body and speech are carried out because of impure motivations of attachment, aggression, ignorance, pride, or jealousy. We should stop the delusion when it first arises in our mind and should stop the unvirtuous actions of body and speech which follow.

In the case of the mahāyāna or bodhisattva vow, delusions are also abandoned, but in a different way. Rather than being rejected, delusions are transformed through the practice of love and compassion. The power of love and compassion gradually increases until it becomes vast and profound when one becomes a bodhisattva. The bodhisattva transforms not only his or her own negative emotions, such as attachment or aggression, but also those of all sentient beings. With the transformation of negative emotions, all delusions are spontaneously abandoned even though some of the actions of a bodhisattva may appear to an observer to transgress the vows, for example, killing or having sexual intercourse. However, internally the motivation for the actions is for the benefit of all sentient beings.

Abandonment of delusion is also the path in the vajrayāna vows. When one is in a state of *meditative absorption* (Skt. *dhyāna*), one comprehends the delusion arising in one's mind and spontaneously liberates oneself from it. This is called *shar drol* in Tibetan in which the delusion arises and is simultaneously liberated.

We should practice all three levels of vows (the prātimokṣha, the mahāyāna and the vajrayāna) at the same time. We should practice the outer discipline of the prātimokṣha in which we have the motivation of liberation for ourselves. Then the inner discipline of the mahāyāna should be practiced and the attitude of the bodhisattva should be adopted. Finally, in the discipline of the vajrayāna, we still meditate on the prātimokṣha and mahāyāna vows, but when we realize the true nature of phenomena, we then practice *yidam meditation*. These are the three-fold vows. An example of someone holding these vows is Milarepa who outwardly did not have the appearance of a fully ordained monk by wearing monk's robes and following all the rules of the Vinaya. However, inwardly his mind was purified of all delusions, and so that is why he was a perfect practitioner. Milarepa said: "I don't know the Vinaya, but taming one's mind is the Vinaya."

In the prātimokṣha, there are three kinds of transgressions: lesser, medium, and greater. The greater transgressions should not be committed. The lesser transgressions occur because we have been conditioned by negative actions carried out during previous lifetimes. Even though we may commit these lesser transgressions, we should not let them accumulate and pile up. Rather, they should be purified or repaired by means of *sojong* (Skt. *poṣhadha*) ceremony. The Tibetan word *so* means "to repair" or "heal" and the word *jong* means to "give up" or "purify." In the sojong ceremony, one is asked if one realizes the faults one has committed and then one promises not to repeat the same mistakes in the future. This process helps one to observe one's vows properly.

After noticing one's faults, one can apply the four powers of antidote. The first is the power of revulsion or regret which is knowing that faults have been committed and being disgusted with them. One can then reject these negativities. The second is the power of remedial action which is knowing the antidotes for unvirtuous actions and then applying them diligently without interruption. The third is the power of reliance which is relying on the three jewels of the Buddha who shows the path, the dharma which is the path of practice, and the saṅgha who are the companions on the path. The fourth is the power to resolve not to repeat the fault in the future. The most important antidotes are the power of regret and the resolve not to repeat the action.

If one commits a fault for the first time, one should resolve not to repeat it; but if one commits the same fault a second time, one should again resolve not to repeat it again and so on. By resolving not to repeat the fault each time one commits a unvirtuous action, one's mind becomes strengthened not to transgress again and in this way *disturbing emotions* (Skt. *kleśhas*) are pacified. This is how the sojong ritual is performed. But purification does not mean that one first commits a fault and then purifies it. What it mean is that by the power of regret one repents one's fault and by the power of antidote one resolves not to fall under the power of disturbing emotions and repeat the fault thereafter. Not being dominated by nonvirtue and delusion, one's mind becomes pacified.

Questions

Question: I wonder what it means in the mahāyāna to transform delusions?

Rinpoche: All delusions of attachment, aggression, and ignorance arise from cherishing oneself, cherishing "I." When practicing the bodhisattva path, instead of cherishing ourselves, we cherish others since we have resolved to work for the benefit of other sentient beings, and in this way, we can transform all the delusions. We have loved and cherished our "I" and have tried to benefit only ourselves since beginningless time. That attitude has been of benefit neither to ourselves nor to others and it has been the cause of our endless wandering in the suffering of saṃsāra. Understanding the faults of cherishing ourselves, we can change the object of the cherishing. Instead of loving ourself, we transform that into love for others, and thus we will be endowed with *loving-kindness*, compassion, and bodhichitta. In this way, we don't focus on the delusions, we don't judge the disturbing emotions as bad, or negative, or wrong. That is why they are transformed naturally.

If we love ourselves and consider ourself important, then aggression will arise because we will have the notion that somebody is harming us, or even that someone such as our parents or friends helping our enemies. So this aggression arises based on valuing ego. But if we change our attitude and are concerned for the welfare of other sentient beings, then the delusions are naturally transformed because we no longer hold ourself as most important.

Question: We start off in the hīnayāna saying, "Don't do these things, they're bad" and then in the mahāyāna we say, "Do these things, they're good." So is the vajrayāna the only way to remove all delusions ultimately?

Rinpoche: Actually, all three vehicles have the way to free us from delusions, but the vajrayāna method is quicker and more powerful.

Question: As I understand it, three of the four antidotes are in the sojong ceremony.

Rinpoche: Actually, only two of the four antidotes are included in the sojong ceremony. These are the power of reliance in which we make our confession in front of all the monks and the power of resolving not to repeat the wrongdoing in the future. The other two powers are not included in the sojong ceremony but are practiced all the time.

Question: It seems that the first power of antidote, the power of regret, would have been included because the preceptor says: "Do you see your faults as a wrongdoing?" and then you have to say, "Yes, I see them as a wrongdoing," and admit what you did. So it seems to me that the first power should be included in the ceremony.

Rinpoche: You actually have the first power within yourself before you make a confession in the sojong. During the ceremony you are asked if you have faults. Although there are four antidotes to practice, only two are included in the sojong ceremony, and the other two should be practiced all the time.

Question: Rinpoche, in the hīnayāna prātimokṣha, you talk about delusions coming up and some sense of suppression of these delusions. Suppression somehow implies that the delusion is not really being dissolved, but is being pushed away so that it actually still exists within one.

Rinpoche: There is no place where the disturbing emotions can dwell in the mind. What suppression means is that one does not allow the delusion to arise in one's mind. śhāntideva gives an example for this. If one tries to destroy one's enemy, then that enemy will go someplace else, and when he is strong enough to take revenge, he will come back to avenge himself. But delusions are very weak; they have no place to go, and no place to come back to. Once they have been removed, they cannot come back again.

Question: Rinpoche said that the lesser transgressions are due to the actions of previous lifetimes. Would Rinpoche please give examples of medium and greater transgressions, and are they also due to actions of previous lifetimes?

Rinpoche: There are two things that have to be abandoned: evil actions and obscurations. If the actions of one's body, speech, or mind cause harm to other beings, either directly or indirectly, these actions are negative or evil deeds. These actions have nothing to do with previous karma or previous habitual tendencies, but rather they are connected with present motivation. Generating the motivation to kill or to steal depends solely on oneself and one has the power to stop oneself from carrying out these negative deeds.

Obscurations, which are related to mind, also do not depend on karma, but depend on one's habitual tendencies. From beginningless time, we have all been habituated with the negative emotions, attachment, aggression, and ignorance. Some people have strong attachment, some have strong aggression, and some have strong ignorance, depending on how much they have been habituated with these delusions. These habitual tendencies are to be abandoned. There are two words that have almost the same meaning in Tibetan. These words are *gom* (spelled in Tibetan as *sgom*), meaning practices or meditation, and *khom* (spelled *goms*) meaning habitual tendencies. When we practice very diligently and our practice is powerful, then that's *gom*, meditation. When we don't practice wholeheartedly, don't put our strength into our practice, then it becomes *khom*, just a habitual tendency. So to abandon obscurations, one has to replace *gom* by *khom*.

Of these three transgressions the lesser transgressions sometimes have not yet ripened into evil deeds but may be the seed of evil deeds later on. For example, some monks don't wear the lower garment, the *sham thab* properly. At that moment, it's not an evil deed, but it may ripen into an actual evil deed gradually.

Question: In vajrayāna post-meditation practice, what is the discipline that self-liberates delusion?

Rinpoche: One should have the two qualities of mindfulness and introspection in post-meditation. The Tibetan equivalent for the English word "post" is *je thop.* The syllable *je* means that one carries the essence of the practice within oneself and should one not lose that essence.

The vajrayāna practice emphasizes the inner mind rather than outer discipline. As Milarepa said: "Taming one's mind is the Vinaya." In order to tame one's mind, one should practice meditation and to have a powerful practice one should depend on mindfulness and introspection.

Question: Could you say something about the secret obstacles?

Rinpoche: In the past, many translators have translated the Tibetan word *sang* as "secret" so the vajrayāna was translated as "the secret mantrayāna." But this is not the proper translation. The short path leading to our destination is called *sang lam,* which means "a short cut" or "a quicker road." So *sang* has the connotation of what is the main issue of the subject. For example, if one wants to put on the light, one has to go and switch it on, you can't do it by fooling with the light bulb. So the main issue of how you can put on the light is called *sang* in Tibetan. When *sang* is translated into English as "secret," it causes a lot of confusion. Take another example of an automobile, the engine is the main key, the most important thing. If you want to drive the car or stop it or whatever, it has to be done by the engine. So the engine is the *sang ba.*

Table 3

The Six Pāramitās

1. Generosity (Skt. *dāna*, Tib. *chinpa*)
2. Discipline (Skt. *śhīla* Tib. *tsultrim*)
3. Patience (Skt. *kṣānti*, Tib. *zod pa*)
4. Exertion (Skt. *vīrya* Tib. *son gu*)
5. Meditation (Skt. *dhyāna*, Tib. *gompa*)
6. Wisdom (Skt. *prajña*, Tib. *sherab*)

The Five Samayas

1. The samaya of Vairocanna (Tib. *rnam par snang mdzad*) which is connected to the buddha family and associated with the wisdom of dharmadhātu (Tib. *chos kyi dbyings kyi ye shes*).
2. The samaya of Akṣhobya (Tib. *mi bskyod pa*) which is connected with the vajra family and associated with the wisdom of mirror-like wisdom (Tib. *me long lti iu' ye shes*).
3. The samaya of Ratnasambhava (Tib. *rin chen 'byung gnas*) which is connected to the jewel family and is associated with wisdom of equanimity (Tib. *mnyan panyid kyi ye shes*).
4. The samaya of Amitābha (Tib. *'od dpag med*) which is connected to the lotus family and is associated with the wisdom of disciminating awareness (Tib. *so sor rtogs pa'i ye shes*).
5. The samaya of Amoghassiddhi (Tib. *don yod grub pa*) which is connected to the karma family and is associated with the wisdom of all-accomplishing action (Tib. *bya ba nan tan du grub ba'a*)

Chapter 6

Nine Aspects of a Noble Being

In the Buddhist tradition there are three different types of practice, namely, view (Tib. *lta ba,* Skt. *darśana*), meditation (Tib. *gom,* Skt. *bhāvanā*), and action (Tib. *spyod pa,* Skt. *caryā*). The *Prātimokṣha* sūtra deals with discipline or action. Living in a monastery or abbey requires discipline. It requires right action which benefits both oneself and other sentient beings for the present and future generations and discipline also maintains the teachings. Noble beings who work for the benefit of other sentient beings, have nine different ways in which they help others; three which are for their own benefit, three which are for the benefit of other sentient beings, and the three last which are both for their own and others' benefit.

Benefiting Oneself

The three ways of working for one's own benefit are hearing (Tib. *thos pa*), contemplating (Tib. *bsam pa*) and meditating (Tib. *gom pa*). One has to depend on someone else to show the right path and so one listens to the teachings of the Buddha. From the hīnayāna point of view the Buddha taught how to free oneself from attachment in the Vinaya and how to free oneself from aggression in the Sūtras and how to free oneself from ignorance in the Abhidharma. This is the Tripiṭaka (literally three baskets) of the hīnayāna. There also exists a Tripiṭaka in the mahāyāna and a Tripiṭaka in the vajrayāna.

The śhāstras or commentaries that help in understanding the Buddha's very vast and profound teachings. The four most important commentaries on the Buddha's teachings are the Madhyamika, the Prajñāpāramitā, the Vinaya and the Abhidharma. The Madhyamika śhāstras deal with emptiness, the Prajñāpāramitā śhāstras deal with knowledge and wisdom, the Vinaya śhāstras deal with discipline or action, and the Abhidharma śhāstras deal with how one progresses along the path.

Having listened to these four treatises, one then contemplates them. One contemplates and examines what one has heard again and again and develops one's knowledge. Finally, one then meditates on these four treatises and the teachings one has received for various practices. Gampopa has said that hearing, contemplating, and meditating should be combined. If a practitioner tries to meditate without having listened to the teachings, he or she cannot meditate because there is nothing to meditate on. It is like a man without hands who tries to climb a mountain. Listening to the teachings without meditating is also not beneficial. It is like a rich man who is a miser and does not buy good food or clothes. Listening to the dharma and meditating is like a bird with two wings who can fly in the sky.

Benefiting Others

The three ways of benefiting other beings are speech (Tib. *mchid*), debate (Tib. *rtsod pa*) and composition (Tib. *rtsom pa*). To convey the real meaning of the teachings to others, one has to speak to them so they can understand. The Buddha said that he was unable to wash away the defilements of others with water. To help sentient beings, one has to show them the right path by explaining the teachings to them. The only way the Buddha could pass on his inner wisdom to others was to talk to them. In a similar manner we also teach others the path by means of speech.

The second way of benefiting others is by debate or discussion. Discussion clears away any doubts or misunderstandings that may arise when the dharma is being explained. The Buddha said that if one wants to buy gold from a shop, before one actually purchases it, one should examine it to see if it is real or fake. Then, if one finds that it is real gold, one should test it to see if it is of good or poor quality by putting it in the fire, cutting it, or rubbing it. By doing so, one finds out if it is pure gold or not. In the same way, the teachings of the Buddha should be carefully examined and analyzed rather than simply accepted. To explain the teachings clearly to others, one should be free of doubt and misunderstanding oneself and this is the function of debate and discussion.

The third way to benefit others is composition. When one is fortunate enough to receive the teachings directly from a teacher, then one can clear away one's doubts and misunderstandings by asking the teacher questions directly. For those who do not have this opportunity, commentaries composed by the great Buddhist masters can be read and studied and thus clarify one's doubts.

Benefiting Self and Others

Finally, there are three ways in which noble beings accomplish the benefit of themselves and others. These are: being learned (Tib. *kha pa*), being well-disciplined (Tib. *tsun pa*), and being kind or compassionate (Tib. *zang po*). It is important to understand the teachings to help all sentient beings. Being learned in the teachings alone is not enough; one should also bring one's learning into the practice. One should also put the prātimokṣha, the bodhisattva, and the vajrayāna vows into practice in order to help other sentient beings. If one brings one's knowledge into the practice, one's example will convince others to practice as well. If one does not practice personally, others will not believe one. For instance, the power of the *garuḍa* protects one from harm caused by the *nāgas,* including catching leprosy.[6] So if a leper claims to have tried the garuḍa's instructions to protect him from the nāgas, nobody will believe him. So to help oneself and other sentient beings, one should be well-disciplined and practice.

The third point is being kind, compassionate. Loving-kindness and compassion are both needed to become a noble being and to help other sentient beings. The manifestation of loving-kindness is not always apparent because it may not manifest itself externally. For example, Marpa was outwardly very unkind to his student Milarepa; he scolded him and abused him by making him undergo so many difficulties. But Milarepa's deep devotion and respect for the teachings prevented him from becoming discouraged. Because of his deep devotion, he obeyed every order Marpa gave him. If Marpa told him to build a house, he built the house; if Marpa told him to demolish the house, he demolished the house. But for other students, the externally manifested loving-kindness and compassion are necessary to bring them to the teachings and the practice.

These nine aspects of a noble being are not actually included in the prātimokṣha but are part of the practice of those who live in monasteries and are the fruition of monastic life.

Questions

Question: Could you explain what nāgas are?
Rinpoche: In general, there are things we can see and things that we cannot see, such as local deities, worldly gods, and

[6]In Tibetan medicine one of the causes of skin diseases especially leprosy is offending a nāga which is a spirit like being which can only be seen by clairvoyant individuals. Lamas are often asked to do a ceremony appeasing the nāgas and the skin conditions can go away.

some sentient beings. Among the nāgas, there are those who practiced the path and attained realization and there are others who through their powerful delusion and aggression misuse their power and harm other sentient beings. Various diseases, such as leprosy, can be caused by these unrealized nāgas.

Question: Is contemplation the same as thinking about something?

Rinpoche: I am not quite sure about the translation for the word "contemplation." The meaning we are using here is to brood over or to think about the teachings we have heard and to try to keep these teachings firmly in our mind by thinking about them again and again. In the sūtras "contemplation" is used for analytical meditation. In England, one translator was using contemplation for all meditation.

Question: In the Japanese tradition there are disciplines like calligraphy, tea ceremony or archery. How does contemplation fit into those practices or traditions?

Rinpoche: Calligraphy and the tea ceremony are good ways to hold the mind, awareness. In the Tibetan tradition, we used to practice putting a small stone in front of us and trying to focus on that stone. Also we practiced mindfulness and awareness by holding the breath, chanting, and prostrating. They are all the same.

Question: Could you give an example of a debate that would go on in a monastery?

Rinpoche: In relation to debate, for instance, there is a group who say that they accept one-pointed emptiness and the reason why there is emptiness is because there is impermanence. If you acknowledge impermanence, then you can accept emptiness. If the reason is false, then you cannot accept emptiness. For example, Rinpoche might say that the hand is empty, and you ask why the hand is empty. Rinpoche would then say, "This is not a hand, this is the thumb, this is the index finger; this is not a hand because this is a nail; this is skin; inside the skin is not a hand but flesh; inside the flesh is not a hand but bone. So there is no hand."

So in the traditional Tibetan way, one makes short simple sentences to debate, so one can debate much quicker. However, the main thing is that there is one thing that has to be accepted. For example, if Rinpoche says the hand is emptiness, then you would ask "why?" Then he would give several reasons to establish the emptiness of the hand. So by debating, one develops confidence in the words and meanings of the philosophical schools.

Chapter 7

Three Aspects of the Bodhisattva Vow

We have discussed monastic discipline from the point of view of the three-fold precepts. The Theravādins observe the precept from the prātimokṣha point of view of self-liberation. From this point of view the Tibetan practitioners seem not to be as strict and literal in observing the *Prātimokṣha Sūtra* as the Theravādins. But since they have the motivation for not only of self-liberation, but also of achieving bodhichitta and maintaining the vows of the vajrayāna as well, the Tibetan practice of the prātimokṣha is more complete.

There might seem to be a contradiction between the practice of the prātimokṣha precepts and the mahāyāna precepts because the former focus on the attainment of self-liberation and the latter on abandoning self-liberation and seeking attainment solely for the benefit of other sentient beings. In Tibet the mahāyāna system consisted of the practice is of the four defeats (Skt. *parajika dharmas*, Tib. *pam pa*), the thirteen remainders (Skt. *samghavashesa dharmas*, Tib. *lhag ma*) and the thirty transgressions (Skt. *naihsargikapayantika dharmas*, Tib. *pong tung*). The rest of the faults were considered to be of lesser importance. But because motivation is regarded as of prime importance, the mahāyāna precepts are regarded as more important. Since an ordinary person had already taken the bodhisattva vow, then when he or she received the prātimokṣha vows, they were viewed from a mahāyāna perspective. So in Tibet the motivation of bodhichitta which arises when one takes the first vows is emphasized, the prātimokṣha vows were not just blindly followed.

The bodhisattva vow has three aspects: abandoning faults; accomplishing virtuous actions; and working for the benefit of all sentient beings. The first precept of abandoning harmful actions of body and speech is the same as the prātimokṣha precept. The second and third precepts, however, are special to the bodhisattva vow and are accomplished by means of the six pāramitās.

The Six Pāramitās

The first pāramitā of generosity has three divisions. The first is to give one's possessions, such as wealth, food, clothing, etc. to others. The second is to protect others from fear and sorrow. According to the mahāyāna system, temporary help, while benefiting other sentient beings, is not as important as ultimate help. To liberate sentient beings ultimately from suffering, one must introduce them to the practice of the dharma, which is the third division, that of giving the noble teachings. The dharma should be presented to beings in accordance with their individual dispositions or inclinations. Some beings are inclined towards the profound teachings, some towards the vast teachings, and some towards the lesser teachings. Some beings may have the inclination to practice the vast and profound teachings, but because of lack of opportunity, they have to practice the lesser teachings. Therefore śhāntideva has said that the vast and profound teachings should not be given to those who do not have the capacity to practice them, and that the lesser teachings should not be given to those who have the ability to practice the vast and profound teachings. Beings should be given teachings in accordance with their ability and capacity.

The second pāramitā is discipline which is to refrain from which has already been talked about. The third pāramitā is patience. This is patience to endure hardship necessary to forebear harm from someone who doesn't like us or one's enemy, to understand the meaning of the teachings, and to accomplish the noble teachings. When our enemy harms us, we normally become angry with him or her. But we should not become angry because it is the nature of ordinary beings to benefit themselves and do harm to others. Therefore, if we relate to an ordinary being, naturally we will be harmed, and that harm is caused by ourself, not by the other. We can take the example of fire. The nature of fire is to be hot and burn, so if we put our hand in the fire and our hand is burned, there is no reason to be angry. It makes no sense to become angry at the fire, the fire will naturally burn us. It is our fault, not the fault of the fire. So if we make a relationship with an ordinary person, we will sometimes receive a harmful response from that person, and so we should develop patience to accomplish virtue. To accomplish virtue we need an object. For example, if we practice generosity, there must be someone to whom we are giving something. In the case of patience, there must be someone towards whom can we practice patience? Not to those who are good to us, but towards those who do not like us or want to harm us. So in order to practice patience, it is necessary to have someone who harms us and doesn't like us helps us accumulate virtue. The third classification of the pāramitā of patience is patience while practicing and realizing the teachings. We should not become discouraged by thinking that we cannot understand or cannot realize the essence of the teachings. We should continue to work with our knowledge and level of practice and put all our effort into practicing with patience.

The fourth pāramitā is diligence. Diligence is necessary because laziness constantly comes up on the path of dharma. One of the aspects of laziness is putting oneself down, thinking that we are hopeless, that we do not have the capacity for realization. This attitude obstructs our practice and our attainment of realization. We should give up thoughts of inadequacy and instead develop the feeling of being able to achieve whatever we want. This is like a good suit of armor that protects us in battle so that we do not fear the enemy; we can have pride in ourself and can rouse up our courage. Similarly, being discouraged is an obstacle on the path of practice which can be overcome by a strong powerful mind. This type of diligence consists of having strong faith and devotion, and turning one's thoughts to the practice of the dharma. The third aspect of diligence is applying one's mind constantly and uninterruptedly to the practice.

The fifth pāramitā is meditation. In general, tranquillity meditation (Skt. *śhamatha*, T: *shinay*) stabilizes and pacifies the mind which is constantly wandering. This pāramitā is of two types, the first being mundane or worldly dhyāna which consists of stabilizing the mind. The second type is transcendent dhyāna in which, based on worldly dhyāna, one's practice and meditative states may progress.

The sixth pāramitā is intelligence or prajna which has the three aspects of hearing, contemplating, and meditating already discussed.

These six pāramitās constitute the foundation for working for the benefit of all sentient beings on the mahāyāna path.

Questions

Question: Rinpoche, I didn't understand the difference between mundane and transcendental meditation. What is an example of worldly meditation?

Rinpoche: Śhamatha meditation is the mundane state of dhyāna. If, in addition to śhamatha, there is the wisdom of egolessness and the practice of insight (vipaśhyanā) meditation that constitutes the transcendental state of dhyāna.

Question: Rinpoche, how useful is it to take the precepts of prātimokṣha? Many of Trungpa Rinpoche's students have been taught in a style that doesn't start with discipline as a function of taking the precepts. Another way of saying it is that if you are already tamed to some extent, then merely keeping the five lay precepts doesn't provoke anything in terms of one's practice. What is the use of having the prātimokṣha vows at all. Also Rinpoche has said that one of the functions of keeping the vows is that you are creating merit for yourself. But the question is, so what?

Rinpoche: Trungpa Rinpoche has been spreading the dharma for sixteen or seventeen years in places where the dharma has never been heard before. Different methods of teaching must be used in places where the dharma has not been spread previously. That is the reason why, for the time being, you are not going through the precepts of the prātimokṣha. That is why a monastery is slowly being established here. Trungpa Rinpoche's idea of building a monastery here is because he sees the importance of practicing the prātimokṣha precepts. In general, it is true that it is most important to tame one's mind which is like a wild elephant. In order to tame our mind, we cannot merely say, "I would like to tame my mind." Different techniques are necessary such as taking the precepts, or mind training (Tib. *lo jong*), and meditation. It would be fine if one could tame one's mind with just one method, but that's not possible.

It is actually difficult to believe that once one has taken the precepts, one's merit is increasing. For example, if one has a hundred animals and kills one animal on each hour then one accumulates the karma of killing an animal each hour. But if one has taken the precept not to kill, then each hour one accumulates the good karma of not killing.

Question: It seems to me that the way Trungpa Rinpoche has taught has emphasized the bodhisattva path, and therefore the way he has presented discipline is in terms of working with the existing situation of life. If you have a family or if you do organizational work connected with the dharma, you have an existing life situation. Rather than changing that life situation by taking the monastic vow and leaving your family, you can accept that situation and make that into a path of discipline in which the five precepts can present some guidance.

Rinpoche: When the Buddha began to spread the dharma, he presented different paths to different people. First he showed the hīnayāna path, then the mahāyāna and gradually he showed the vajrayāna path. Trungpa Rinpoche was doing the same thing. He came to a place where dharma had not been heard before and began to spread the dharma. At first he taught his students the practice of śhamatha, then gradually the practice of the *four preliminaries* (Tib. *ngondro)* and gradually the practice of Vajrayoginī. Then gradually he built a monastery.

Chapter 8

The Five Classes of Vajrayāna Precepts

There are four methods to bring sentient beings onto the path of dharma. The first method is to provide whatever is needed. With the motivation of helping others to attain enlightenment, others can be brought to the path of dharma by being shown the right method. The second is with kind speech; when others are brought to the path, their faith may be aroused by speaking kind words. If these two methods are based on impure motivation, they do not help; if they are supported by pure motivation, they are the perfect method; and if they are further supported by the precepts of bodhichitta, they are even more extraordinary and beneficial. The third method is to communicate directly through the teachings, showing those who have already been introduced to the dharma the proper path of practice and eradicating whatever obstacles may arise while they are practicing the path. These obstacles may cause the practitioner to lose faith and devotion so one can eliminate the practitioner's obstacles. If the practitioner has gone off onto the wrong path, one can guide him or her back to the right path, and if that person is not evolving on the path, one can help them to evolve. The fourth method is to act appropriately with the ways of the world. For example one should practice in the same way that one explains the dharma to others.

The prātimokṣha vows are called the outer precepts in which one refrains from destructive actions of body and speech. The bodhichitta precepts of the mahāyāna are called the inner precepts in which one examines the mind.

The third stage is called the "secret vajrayāna" precepts. The word *sang ba* is usually translated into English as "secret," but this has an ambiguous interpretation. It's as if Tibetan Buddhism has to conceal its practice because there is something wrong in its practices. This misconception is due to the way the words *sang ba* has been translated. In all the Buddhist practices, particularly in the vajrayāna practices, there is nothing that must be hidden and kept secret. There is no fault in the practice that makes it improper to show to others. Nor are Tibetan Buddhists greedy and don't want to reveal the teachings to others. Not giving the teachings to others, is not in accord with the dharma. The word *sang ba* instead has the connotation of "pointing to the main issue," and gives the idea of something powerful. At the mahāyāna level, the main issue according to the sūtras is emptiness which is empty and has the aspect of clarity. At the vajrayāna level of *sang ba* the main issue is one's inner mind, not emptiness. For example, if a sleeping man dreams about a tiger, giving him weapons or getting his friends to help him are of no use. The only way to help him is to awaken him from his sleep and then instantly he will be free of his fear the tiger. Similarly, if we can awaken from our inner mind, we find that there is no essence in external phenomena.

When we examine our inner mind, we find that it is polluted by the five disturbing emotions (Skt. *kleśha*; Tib. *nyon mong)*: attachment, aggression, ignorance, jealousy, and pride. When these five emotions are purified, they are called wisdoms (Skt. *jñāna*; Tib. *yeshe*). When we realize the nature of our mind as the same as the five wisdoms, we will then manifest the five wisdoms. This process of trying to find the main issue of the mind is called *sang ba* or the "secret" vajrayāna.

These vajrayāna precepts are divided into five classes according to the five buddha families. The first precept is the *samaya* of Vairocana which consists, as we have already described of the path of the three activities of a bodhisattva: refraining from unvirtuous deeds, accomplishing virtue, and working for the sake of all sentient beings. Vairocana is the foundation of the other buddha families, and the wisdom of the *dharmadhātu* is regarded as the foundation of all the wisdoms.

The second, the purification of aggression into mirror-like wisdom is the samaya of Akṣhobya which consists of always holding the vajra and ritual bell and having devotion to and faith in one's root guru. The delusion of aggression is very powerful and in order to purify this, one must depend on one's root guru. Aggression is transformed by the mirror-like wisdom into pacification.

The third, the samaya of Ratnasambhava, transforms pride into the wisdom of equanimity which enriches. The practice for this samaya is generosity with regard to wealth, possessions, food, etc.

The fourth, the samaya of Amitabha, transforms attachment into the wisdom of discriminating awareness. Its activity is that of magnetizing other sentient beings, and to accomplish this one must observe the three-fold precepts of hīnayāna, mahāyāna, and vajrayāna. Having the knowledge of the three *yānas*, one can show others the path appropriate to their individual disposition.

The fifth, the samaya of Amoghasiddhi which transforms jealousy into the wisdom that accomplishes all actions. The activity in this family is that of wrathful action. By making offerings of tormas to the wrathful deities, one can accomplish one's goal faster.

The precepts of the hīnayāna are included in those precepts of the mahāyāna which in turn are included in the vajrayāna precepts. Therefore to observe the vajrayāna precepts is to observe all three yānas at once.

Questions

Question: When you spoke of the samaya of Akṣobya, you were speaking about the purification of anger, and then in the samaya of Amoghasiddhi you spoke about wrathful activity. Could you say how those two, anger and wrath, are different?
Rinpoche: The deities have two aspects, peaceful and wrathful. The peaceful aspect is like the bodhisattvas. The wrathful aspect is not in the form of delusion such as aggression, but rather the wrathful activity helps one to accomplish one's goal rapidly. So wrathfulness and aggression are different. The wrathful aspect has power. For example, if a child does something dangerous and if his parents pet him and says "Don't do that," the child won't listen to them. But if the parents raise a stick and say, "Don't do that," then the child will obey. The wrathful action of raising the stick has the power to stop the child from doing dangerous things which a peaceful method does not have. That action is not the method of aggression but rather the method of wrathful activity. Aggression in the purified state is mirror-like wisdom, the activity of which is pacification. Jealousy in the purified state is all-accomplishing wisdom, the activity of which is wrathful action. That is why aggression and wrathfulness are different.
Question: Rinpoche, how does the offering of tormas relate to that?
Rinpoche: The offerings and tormas are offered to the dharmapālas, so that is how someone's goal is quickly attained.
Question: When practicing guru yoga, do you rouse confidence?
Rinpoche: Yes.
Question: So if your guru is three hundred miles away from you, but if you pray to him, how would you get results?
Rinpoche: If you meditate, you create a visualization and it seems to be part of the visualization that you believe in it.

But obviously the visualization is not reality in the common sense because it's a created reality. In my practice, I'm creating that maṇḍala within my mind, and I don't think about whether it exists out there or not.

The visualization is related to reality. For example, if you visualize the guru on the top of your head, that will be of benefit to you. If you visualize a frog on top of your head, that will be of no benefit. When we visualize, we need some foundation on which we can visualize, therefore we visualize on the foundation of tormas.

Question: Rinpoche, when you discussed the padma family and the transformation into discriminating awareness, it seems to me that you have to really understand and practice all three yānas completely.

Rinpoche: One doesn't have to practice all three yānas in detail. By practicing vajrayāna, one is practicing all three yānas because the hīnayāna precepts are included in the mahāyāna, and the mahāyāna precepts are included in the vajrayāna. By realizing the three yānas, when one teaches, one can give teachings appropriate to different individuals. The Buddha gave 84,000 different teachings, but that doesn't mean that one has to go through all 84,000 of them. If one practices fully one of them, that serves the purpose of practicing all the rest of them. Since each sentient being has differing dispositions and capabilities, there are 84,000 different teachings. That is also why that there are three yānas.

Question: Would the practice of Vajrayoginī be one of the 84,000?

Rinpoche: Yes, that is one path of the vajrayāna included in the 84,000 teachings of the Buddha.

Question: What is the practice for the samaya of Vairocana? You said there were three precepts of Vairocana and I was wondering what they are.

Rinpoche: The samaya of Vairocana is the precepts of the bodhisattva and the fruit of that is dharmadhātu which is the foundation of all the activities, pacification, magnetizing, accomplishing, and enriching.

Question: I used to believe that this wall was more real than something like Vajrayoginī which I couldn't even imagine. So because of the effect of that belief, whether Vajrayoginī is real or not real is actually not important, but the effect of Vajrayoginī and offering to Vajrayoginī is important.

Rinpoche: That's very good if you have the confidence of visualizing or realizing Vajrayoginī as solid as this wall, more real than the wall. The effect of that is positive, very good. The wall, like all phenomena, is empty. But according to ultimate truth, Vajrayoginī is real and exists from the point of view of Shentong Madhyamika. Ultimately all forms do exist. Since you have that attitude, and by realizing ultimate truth, you can attain your goal very fast.

Question: A teacher, not a Buddhist teacher, once said that you could take anything and put it up on a shrine and venerate it and by generating your own energy into that situation, it would become sacred. If you just sit yourself down to work with the practice and believe it has validity, then it has validity. How is that separated from your own belief in some sort of actual validity that exists beyond whether you believe it or not?

Rinpoche: Not seeing something is not sufficient reason for saying that it doesn't exist. For instance two people may be sitting facing each other and they can see each other, but they cannot see what the other one is thinking about. The reason why we offer torma and other offerings is to show that we have confidence, devotion, and conviction in the deities to whom we are making the offerings. Whether it is to our root guru or our yidam, the most important thing is confidence. If we have no confidence, we will never accomplish our goal. Also we should have confidence in the personal deities and dharmapālas and make offerings to them, because they have the power of eliminating our suffering. It's not that the gods are hungry or something like that.

Question: These dharmapālas are states of mind, aren't they?

Rinpoche: According to the Hindu point of view, everything was created by a god, but we don't believe that. The Theravāda school emphasizes that there is no god at all and that is also true from the vajrayāna point of view. Also from the vajrayāna point of view, happiness and sorrow all depend on oneself. Yet an infinite numbers of buddhas and bodhisattvas exist, some in the form of personal deities and some in the form of dharma protectors (Skt. *dharmapālas*). If we arouse faith and devotion to them, through their power we can receive their blessings. That is why the yidams and dharmapālas are not just the creation of one's mind.

Question: My question is that with these torma offerings, there is sometimes the feeling, "Am I a blind believer if I do that, just believing that blessings come to me? How can that be reasonable? Am responding to blessings coming from outside which I do not see? How do I know that I receive blessings?"

Rinpoche: The offering is important. For example, there are two friends who have a very close and deep relationship with love and compassion for each other. But merely saying it is not sufficient. They must express their love and compassion to each other either by exchanging gifts or by helping each other. In the same way, to say, "I have very deep faith and devotion to the Buddha" is not enough. You must offer something to represent your deep faith in the Buddha. In some ways it is difficult to understand how we receive blessings, but in other ways it is quite easy. For instance, when we see the statue of the Buddha or a shrine, devotion arises within us. But, for instance, when that couple came here to make the film for TV and saw the shrine, they just said, "Oh, this is a colorful picture. It must be some sort of superstition that they believe in." Although we see the same objects, the way we see it and the way they see it is different. They don't understand what it is. So these are the blessings that we are receiving.

Question: Sometimes we make offerings and we see the ravens sitting outside. Then somebody says: "Oh, the mahākālas are outside" and everybody says: "Oh, the mahākālas are outside." So I ask what is this all about?

Rinpoche: One cannot say that all the ravens we see outside eating tormas are all mahākālas. Usually they are just ravens, but sometimes, depending on one's motivation and one's power of faith in the raven, it will produce blessings.

Chapter 9
The Vows of the Three Yānas

The subject of our talk is the three vows (Tib. *dom sum*). But in order to understand fully the meaning of the three vows, we should first see the significance and auspiciousness of Trungpa Rinpoche who was a special being, not an ordinary being like ourselves. Special beings have the capacity to plan how they take birth and how they die and how they spend the period between their birth and death. Whatever plans they make, they carry out to completion. In contrast, we as ordinary beings have no control of how we are born or how we die.

For example, His Holiness the sixteenth Karmapa chose the perfect time to be born, namely, when his teachers Situ Rinpoche, Pema Wangchuk Gyalpo, Jamgon Rinpoche, and Palden Öser were old enough to look after and transmit the sacred teachings. His Holiness also had awareness that overwhelming changes would occur in Tibet and that it would be necessary to establish the dharma in India and Europe and North America. Based on his omniscience, he chose to be reborn at a time when he would receive the complete transmission from his teachers who themselves were elderly and when he himself would be old enough to take on the full responsibility of cultivating the seed of dharma throughout the world. It would have been very difficult for his elderly teachers to leave Tibet. Therefore they left their bodies and reincarnated in a new body which allowed them to escape easily. These are the extraordinary qualities of special beings. If we look back, it seems as if he planned all these occurrences, although at the time no one could understand the reasons for his actions. Moreover, right after leaving Tibet His

Holiness immediately established Rumtek monastery and passed on all the transmissions to the four regents (who were his four reincarnated teachers mentioned above). When he knew that they were strong enough to take on the responsibility in the East and West, His Holiness passed into nirvāṇa in 1981. So His Holiness completed everything and left nothing incomplete. All this seems completely planned: when to take rebirth, what activities to carry out, and having completed the activities, when to leave. These are the buddha activities of special beings. It is similar with Trungpa Rinpoche. Trungpa Rinpoche's main activity has been the cultivation of the *buddhadharma* on the soil of America. Everyone knows that he is an outstanding teacher, and because of his skill and wisdom, he learned the correct means of cultivating the teachings in the minds of Westerners. He taught his students the buddhadharma starting with śhamatha where one concentrates one's mind on the breath, and then he gradually introduced the vajrayāna practices including Vajrayoginī, Chakrasaṃvara, and mahāmudrā. Having given his students enough education and all the requirements for the empowerments in the higher practices and knowing that his students had the capability to take on responsibility, he died, leaving no part of his work incomplete. I believe that all of Trungpa Rinpoche's students are taking on that responsibility and are working according to his instructions and intentions. Through his skillfulness, Trungpa Rinpoche saw that it was necessary to establish a traditional monastery in America and from that Gampo Abbey came into existence.

In Tibet, after Buddhism was introduced during the time of King Songsen Gampo, but it was not strongly established until five generations had gone by. Then śhāntarakṣhita was invited to come to Tibet. To decide whether the Tibetans were really able to maintain and adjust to strict monastic discipline, the full ordination vows were given only to seven students as a test. Finding that these Tibetan monks were able to adjust to the rules and discipline, the ordination was made widely available. Although it took five generations in Tibet to establish monasticism, here in America Trungpa Rinpoche has achieved this within one lifetime.

The vows are maintained by adjusting to the rule (Tib. *tsul*) or the discipline (Tib. *tsultrim*). The way to adjust to the discipline is knowing the three vows. Outwardly one adjusts to the śhrāvaka vows, inwardly to the bodhisattva vows, and secretly one maintains the vajrayāna vows. It should be very clear that to maintain complete discipline, one must maintain all three vows. This is known as "the vajra-holder who keeps the three vows" or *sumten dorje dzinpa* in Tibetan. In regard to the outer discipline of the rules, the Theravādins believe that Tibetan Buddhism does not maintain the rules as completely and as precisely as the Theravādins in, for example, the way of washing the begging bowl or the way of folding the dharma robe. It is true that in Tibetan Buddhism particular vows are not emphasized as much.

It is human nature to feel, "If I accomplish this one wish, I will feel quite satisfied." But when that wish has been satisfied, one becomes more desirous, more ambitious. Since there is no end to the desires of the mind and no way to satisfy it, the Buddha said that one must discipline one's mind in the very beginning.

Among the disciplines, there is the *sojong, yarne,* and the *gagne* ceremonies. In the word *sojong,* the syllable *so* means "to renew" and *jong* means "to purify or confess." So the significance of the sojong ceremony is the renewing of one's vows through a confession. This does not mean that one can carry out negative actions of body, speech, and mind and then simply be absolved of the negative karma by the sojong ceremony. Sojong is traditionally done twice a month and during that period one tries to examine how mindful one has been in body, speech, and mind. One rejoices if one finds, on examination, that one has maintained all the disciplines of body, speech, and mind. But if one finds that any of the disciplines have been broken, then such a breach is purified and the vows are renewed. When the Buddha was about to pass away, he told his monks that the *Prātimokṣha* Sūtra would be the sole liberator for them, meaning that if one applies the vows according to the instruction given in this sūtra, it would be like a guide that can liberate one.

During the period of the summer retreat or yarne (Tib. *yar* means "summer" and *ne* means "location") one examines one's feelings and reactions within the atmosphere of strict discipline. Immediately following yarne is the gagye (Tib. for "stopped") in which the discipline is loosened and one examines oneself physically and mentally within the atmosphere of the loosened discipline.

The outer discipline of the śhrāvaka leading to individual liberation (Tib. *so sor tharpa*) is the path of abandoning the defilements of body and speech. Actions of body and speech incite the disturbing emotions. When one's actions of body and speech are based on discipline, they do not arouse the disturbing emotions but remain free from them. In that sense the vows of the śhrāvakas is the path of abandoning the kleśhas. In the inner discipline of the bodhisattva path consists of transforming these disturbing emotions to positive qualities. In the secret discipline of the vajrayāna, the disturbing emotions themselves are regarded as the path towards experiencing wisdom. So by working with all three techniques of abandoning the kleśhas, transforming the kleśhas, and taking the kleśhas as path, one can realize the fruition of primordial wisdom (Skt. *jñāna*, Tib. *yeshe*).

Questions

Question: Rinpoche, you said that it was very important to integrate all three vows. If we integrate these three and if we abandon the kleśhas, what is there left to transform?

Rinpoche: Unfortunately, our kleśhas are very strongly rooted within us and so it's not as easy as simply saying, "I want to abandon my kleśhas" and the kleśhas are gone. Even though we want to abandon the kleśhas, they remain with us. To completely eliminate the kleśhas, we must go from one method to another. Though we may want to simply transform the kleśhas into wisdom, we are unable to do so. Or, when we want to regard the kleśhas as the path to enlightenment, we find that we are not developed enough to do so. Since the kleśhas are so deeply and powerfully rooted, we must apply these three different vows one by one to achieve our goal.

Generally, we really try to alternate the different methods of eliminating the kleśhas. It is similar to when one is sick and takes medicine and tries other means to eliminate the disease. But we can also look at it like we are applying the methods simultaneously. Externally we are maintaining the discipline, internally we are maintaining the bodhisattva vows, and we are practicing the vajrayāna. Are we doing it all at the same time? You could do it if you're careful.

Question: In the discussion so far we have talked about dealing with conflicting emotions and abandoning or transforming or taking the kleśhas as path. If we can deal with the problem of the conflicting emotions or the kleśhas, then the basic root issue of the ego process is also dealt with.

Rinpoche: Ego-clinging is the root of all the kleśhas, so one could safely say that the three vows are to abandon ego-clinging, to transform ego-clinging, and to take ego-clinging itself as path.

As one becomes more skillful in applying the methods of abandoning, transforming, and regarding the kleśhas as path, one also develops wisdom which means cutting through the two obscurations.

Question: It's easier to understand how the vows work with the kleśhas of attachment and aggression, but how do they work with ignorance?

Rinpoche: Of all the kleśhas, attachment and aggression are very distinct and the most powerful ones. When we work with the pacifying of passion and aggression and then the incitement of these two kleśhas is absent, the mind experiences stability, clarity, and goodness. Based on that, it becomes very simple to work towards the elimination of ignorance. For example, when we practice meditation and let our mind become distracted, then we experience either intolerable agitation or tremendous drowsiness. But if, at the very beginning of our sitting meditation, we discipline our mind so that it does not become distracted, then we experience these two obstacles much less.

Question: What is the kleśha of ignorance actually? Sometimes it's considered to be one of the three root kleśhas and sometimes it's considered simply as basic ignorance.

Rinpoche: In Tibetan, the word *ti mug* means "ignorance" and there is also the Tibetan word *ma rigpa* which means "a blindness," or the opposite of awareness. These two terms are used in the Abhidharma with the first being referred to as "mixed ignorance" and the second being referred to as "unmixed ignorance." Mixed ignorance (*ti mug*) is something that comes together with any of the other kleśhas, such as attachment or aggression. The moment the attachment arises, the ignorance is there with it. So this mixed ignorance is inseparable from the kleśhas. The unmixed ignorance (*ma rigpa)* is quite different. With no knowledge of meditation, no knowledge of dharmadhātu or dharmatā, that lack of knowledge, which is a state of confusion, is unmixed ignorance.

Question: There seems to be a distinction between meditation and post-meditation. In post-meditation, we seem to have the idea that things exist which probably is the ignorance of dharmatā. Is it possible to overcome that ignorance in post-meditation or is that only possible only in meditation?

Rinpoche: We must distinguish clearly between the meditation of an ordinary person and that of an exalted being. As an ordinary person, we have no actual experience of dharmadhātu or dharmatā so they become for us, simply symbolic examples on which we meditate. Then in our post-meditation, we try to carry on whatever feeling or experience we have had in our meditation on the symbolic example. An exalted being (that is a bodhisattva on the first bodhisattva level) has the actual realization of dharmadhātu or dharmatā and does not have to dwell upon the symbolic examples. This person can maintain the feeling of the experience of dharmatā in post-meditation with the certainty of mind. As a beginner, we refer back to whatever experience we have had in our meditation session, but as we develop, there comes to be no distinction between meditation and post-meditation; both experiences are the same.

Question: Since the kleśhas are so powerfully rooted we need all three vows or disciplines and can practice them alternately or simultaneously. Would a Theravādin śhrāvaka say that the kleśhas could be uprooted with just the and mindfulness?

Rinpoche: A śhrāvaka works with abandoning the kleśhas. By strong discipline of body and speech, and not permitting body or speech to arouse or incite the kleśhas, the kleśhas are weakened and pacified. At the same time the śhrāvaka's capacity to rest in the meditative state develops.

Question: Would this be ground from a vajrayāna point of view as opposed to fruition from the Theravādin point of view?

Rinpoche: In the vajrayāna practice, emphasis is also placed on maintaining the discipline of the śhrāvaka because if the kleśhas are pacified by means of the śhrāvaka vows, then one is able to preserve in a very wholesome way whatever further precepts or vows that are made, such as the bodhisattva vows or the vajrayāna vows. One can achieve complete elimination of the kleśhas by means of śhrāvaka practice alone without the mahāyāna or vajrayāna, but since one is applying only one method and not several, it will take longer and it will be more difficult.

Chapter 10
The Vows of the Śhrāvakas

The observing of the three disciplines of the three levels of practice or yānas strictly is a very effective practice. But strictly and seriously practicing and preserving the vajrayāna samayas (Tib. *dam tsig*), includes the precepts of the other two yānas.

In more detail, the precepts of the śhrāvakas are known in Sanskrit as the prātimokṣha (Tib. *so sor tharpa*) which means "individual liberation." So this liberation is not the ultimate liberation, but by maintaining this discipline one liberates and separates oneself from temporary uncomfortable difficulties. This discipline from the ordinary point of view seems to be a hard task and a burden, but the truth, if we do not maintain this discipline, we actually experience worse hardships over longer periods of time. So by keeping the prātimokṣha vows, we become free from these difficulties in life. If we can keep one precept that eliminates one problem; if we can keep two precepts, that eliminates two problems, and so on.

Sometimes it is thought that the prātimokṣha vows are observed only by fully ordained monks and nuns, but this is not the case. Usually we speak of five precepts, but sometimes there are seven or eight precepts. These five basic precepts are included within the monastic vows of fully ordained monks and nuns and three of the precepts are included within the lay person's vows or *genyen* vows. For the householder or lay practitioner, there are two categories of precepts: temporary (Tib. *du tim)* vows and permanent (Tib. *ten tim*) vows. If the householder decides to keep the vows for their entire lifetime, that is a permanent vow. However, because householders often have jobs and a household and a family to look after, they do not have enough time to fully devote their life to practice. It is difficult for them to maintain permanent commitments. So the householder can accumulate merit by observing the genyen vows for one day, two days and so on. Keeping the vows very strictly during those periods is known as "the commitments of time."

Similarly, the monastic ordinations are given in a step by step process with a gradually increasing numbers of precepts. First there are the ordinary ordination vows (Tib. *barma rabjung)* then there are the novice vows (Tib. *getsul* and *getsulma*), and finally there are the full ordination vows (Tib. *gelong* or *gelongma)* which leads one towards liberation.

The main idea of ordination is to overcome the emotional obscurations by developing mindfulness and alertness. One of the ways that monastics train themselves in mindfulness and alertness is with the clothes that they wear which are designed not to fit their body. The literal translation for the dharma robe is "made in a square shape." For example the dharma robe (Tib. *chogo*) does not fit to the body and falls off very easily, so the person must be constantly mindful not to let it slip off and to hold onto the edge or corner of the robe at all times. Also the color and shape of the robes are much different from that of lay people which again acts as a constant reminder to monks and nuns that they are different from lay people because they have to maintain the prātimokṣha vows. Again the purpose of this is to develop mindfulness. Another example is the begging bowl which can't be made to have a flat bottom so that it sits on the table firmly. Instead it has a round bottom and one must maintain constant alertness to keep it from spilling.

The basic idea of this is to preserve the commitment of the four root vows and to learn not to be involved in the transgressions. To be effective in these two, one must examine one's life very carefully to see whether one is breaking any of these vows with one's body, speech, or mind. It is crucial to do this if one has taken these vows. To maintain mindfulness and alertness, one has to be careful that one is not indulging in the obscurations of attachment, aggression, pride, and so forth. As a sign of commitment, whenever one talks to someone, one must be mindful of what one is talking about and how one is behaving physically. One has to be mindful of all actions. By virtue of this mindfulness and alertness, the conflicting emotions decrease and weaken and when this happens there are fewer obstacles in meditation that can hinder one's samādhi. When this happens, the *creation stage* and the *completion stage* of meditation becomes very clear, precise, and uninterrupted and there is the experience of relaxation. These then are the fruition of observing discipline.

Traditionally, it is said that keeping the physical commitments will lead to the ability to keep the verbal commitments. This means that the result of keeping the physical commitments causes one to indulge less in the negative actions of speech which in turn helps in keeping the verbal commitments. If one learns to keep the verbal commitments, this in turn helps one to maintain the mental commitments. So by first concentrating on the physical aspects of the vows, one can develop the verbal and the mental aspects of the vows. By keeping all three commitments, the fully ordained gelong or gelongma will be led towards liberation. The Buddha taught the development of discipline, meditative absorption, and wisdom (Skt. *śhīla*, *samādhi*, and *prajñā*). Discipline is the ground for both wisdom and meditative concentration. Because of discipline one experiences peacefulness in addition to mindfulness and alertness. Discipline helps to bring meditative absorption from which wisdom develops. This wisdom is the realization of the egolessness of phenomena. Discipline alone is not sufficient to bring the realization of nature of egolessness, but śhīla and samādhi together assist in the fruition of prajñā which experiences the egolessness or selfless nature.

The group of practitioners who are practicing discipline is known as the saṅgha. The commitments of the saṅgha are twofold. First, the saṅgha tries not to show disrespect to any of the Buddha's teachings, and second, the saṅgha tries to act in accordance with wholesome and harmonious behavior. The saṅgha members are known as having a "common taste," because they have all received the same precepts and are all committed to working towards the same goal of pacifying the emotional obscurations. Having taken the same commitments, if an individual commits disharmony in the saṅgha and is disrespectful to the saṅgha, it is a breach of the refuge vow.

The Four Trainings

Another aspect of discipline is the four trainings of virtuous dharma. The first of these may be translated as "Don't return anger with anger" which means that even if one of the saṅgha members should become aggressive or angry towards you, you must not react with anger but be tolerant and patient. It is important to realize that the aggressive and angry person has, in this circumstance, lost his mindfulness and alertness. If you maintain your own mindfulness and alertness and try to be kind and gentle, that will help the other person to regain his or her understanding of the importance of mindfulness and alertness and thus help that person not to indulge in conflicting emotions so you have reminded him or her to be mindful and alert.

The second training of virtuous dharma which concerns direct speech is, "Don't return harsh words with harsh words" which means that if a saṅgha member speaks very critically of you, you shouldn't become angry and return the harsh words. Rather you should try to be patient and maintain your mindfulness and alertness. As a result of not reacting to the other person's rebuke, the other person's wish to harm decreases and your own kleśhas decrease as well making this of great benefit to self and others.

The third training of virtuous dharma is similar to the second, but concerns indirect speech which is offensive in a very subtle way, such as hinting a criticism. So the training is "Don't return criticism with criticism" meaning one does not to return any offensive gesture or comment, but retains mindfulness and alertness.

The fourth training of virtuous dharma is literally, "If struck, don't strike back." Even if a person tries to harm you physically, it is important not to retaliate, but to maintain mindfulness and alertness. In this way you actually subdue the kleśha of anger by means of tolerance.

As we practice these disciplines, we must learn not to fall into the two extremes: indulgence or asceticism. The extreme of indulgence means that we are so attached to name, fame, possessions, and luxury that we are never satisfied with what is acquired. We may need more and more clothes, more and more possessions, and even when we have them, one still desires more. Our mind is never satisfied. We must learn to be content with whatever clothes, wealth, or possessions we have. The extreme of asceticism means that, like some non-Buddhist practitioners, we believe that by torturing the physical body with heat, cold, hunger, or thirst, we can attain realization. This is incorrect because realization can actually be experienced only by means of discipline, meditation, and wisdom.

However, if we can remain free from grasping and clinging, then even though we take the vows, we can enjoy such things as living in a luxurious home, wearing expensive clothes, eating fancy food, and so on. We do not have to reject such things, if they have been provided to us. If we can have all this abundance without having to work hard throughout our entire life, then we have the right to enjoy it, provided we do not cling to it. On the other hand, if such wealth, food and luxury is not within our reach, you must not crave it. We must learn to live simply. When we have it, enjoy it; when we don't have it, do not long for it.

Questions

Question: There are a number of cultural differences between East and West. I wonder if Rinpoche could tell us how he informs his monks of the proper attitude to take when first taking the vows.

Rinpoche: Yes, there is a difference in culture between the East and the West, but with respect to the practice, there is no difference between them. Both East and West must adopt the same practice. So when you are receiving the full ordination, the main point to bear in mind is that you are not doing it for someone else, you are doing it to subdue your own kleśhas and in order to do so, it is necessary to develop mindfulness and awareness. By cultivating mindfulness and awareness, you learn to be satisfied with what you have and aim towards the development of samādhi which brings prajñā.

However, the prātimokṣha vow of the śhrāvaka differs from the prātimokṣha vow of the mahāyāna. As explained earlier, the goal of the prātimokṣha vow of the śhrāvaka is individual liberation. Having experienced the vicious state of saṃsāra you are practicing the discipline to liberate yourself from that pain and misery. On the other hand, in the prātimokṣha vow of the mahāyāna, you practice the discipline of mindfulness and awareness to become capable of benefiting other sentient beings in the future.

Question: There might be attitudes peculiar to Westerners that lead us astray from the possibility of mindfulness and awareness, for example, the idea of discipline. Often when we speak of discipline we think of something imposed from the outside, whereas the Buddhist notion of discipline is that it is willingly undertaken.

Rinpoche: It is really not very helpful to discuss individual viewpoints or cultural feelings. The Buddha himself did not command his disciples to obey the vows. Rather, he presented the reason for the vows and showed what kinds of suffering we experience if we do not keep the vow. Based on this reasoning, we learn that by keeping the vows, we become free from suffering, and by not keeping them we are subject to the miseries of saṃsāra. Understanding that, we take the vow which should not be regarded as something compulsory or an order from some superior being. Receiving the ordination cannot be done without understanding and learning about the vows. All the high Tibetan teachers have always made it clear to their students that the precepts must be taken voluntarily with full knowledge of what they entail. We must not regard the precepts as a burden, rather we must understand that by keeping the precepts, suffering is eliminated. Therefore the vows are a joy rather than a hardship. This is the attitude we must develop before receiving the commitments.

Question: I find it very difficult to work with anger because it is so fast. The other kleśhas involve a little time for thinking whereas anger seems to come out and the harmful results appear immediately. How does one avoid saying harmful things? It seems that I have the intention to avoid it, but before I know it, it's there and the harm is done.

Rinpoche: There are various methods to overcome anger: the vajrayāna method, the mahāyāna method, and the hīnayāna method. Anger or aggression is very fast acting and very powerful, and from the prātimokṣha point of view, one really can't do very much at that very moment. But one can rain oneself in beforehand. In daily life when one is not angry or offended or being criticized, one is physically and mentally peaceful and can keep repeating mentally, "Even if I am offended or criticized, becoming angry is not positive." At the beginning, even though one has that fresh idea of the negative aspect of one's anger, one might lose one's temper when the circumstance occurs that someone is criticizing one. But one's anger may not be as strong as before. Maybe one still becomes angry, but one's words will be less harsh than if one had never practiced this method. So the first time one may not be too successful, but the second time or third time it might improve, and that is how one gradually evolves. The most important thing is never to give up. The worst thing that one can do is to doubt that the practice can work and stop practicing. So never give up. Keep on practicing.

Question: Would you please clarify the difference between the term used for the prātimokṣha vows and the vajrayāna samaya?

Rinpoche: In Tibetan, there are two terms, *dam tsig* and *dom pa*. Here *dam* means "tight," and *tsig* means "word," and *dom pa* is a verb meaning "to bind." The syllable *dam* also has the connotation of sacredness. I feel that the term *damtsig* should be reserved for the vajrayāna samaya. The word *dompa* can be thought of as the binding force of discipline.

Question: My second question is about the lineage of the different vows. In terms of the prātimokṣha, there are the usual five precepts for the lay person, the pancashila, plus the additional three making up the ashtashila, which include not wearing jewelry, not watching theatrical displays, and not sleeping in a high bed. Then there are the dashashila, the ten wholesome actions of body, speech and mind mentioned in Gampopa's *The Jewel Ornament of Liberation* and by Jamgon Kongtrul. I was wondering why the dashashila are not administered as vows.

Rinpoche: As we discussed earlier, a lay person may take the precepts either permanently or for a given period of time. A householder is able to keep the five precepts or sometimes four in a permanent manner, which are called the permanent vows. But it is rather difficult for a lay person to keep the other precepts like not wearing jewelry and not indulging in singing and dancing because these are ways of socializing in the lay community. But the lay person can maintain the five precepts, or the four, on a permanent foundation. The temporary vow, which is given for a day or two can be strictly preserved by the lay person, because for a limited period of time, the householder is able to avoid wearing jewelry, singing and dancing, etc. The five and eight vows for the lay person are all related to physical and verbal discipline. The ten unwholesome actions, however, include envy, harmful thoughts, and heretical views. In the ten vows, a person is not sufficiently spiritually advanced on the śhrāvaka level to maintain these mental disciplines as a vow. Therefore to vow to refrain from these three unwholesome mental actions as a vow, one would be bound to break them. That is why one does not take them as a vow.

The aspect of refraining from unwholesome speech includes refraining from creating disharmony, refraining from idle gossip, and refraining from the use of inappropriate or harsh words. For a lay person it is often quite natural to participate in gossip and within the family and other worldly activities one occasionally indulges in harsh words. So these three are not regarded as commitments or vows. For the lay person, the vow is simply not to tell lies.

Question: So the ten unwholesome actions to refrain from are given not as vows or precepts, but as a teaching so that people could have the aspiration to keep them.

Rinpoche: Yes. The ten wholesome and ten unwholesome actions are taught so that students will develop their knowledge and, by mindfulness and alertness, avoid participating in all the unwholesome actions. The precepts are given as a foundation and beyond that foundation, the ten unwholesome actions are situations which one tries to learn to avoid by simply being mindful. If they were given as vows, it becomes very inconvenient because they are experienced so often in lay life.

Question: Rinpoche, in the ordination vows of *barma rabjung* are there five vows or seven or eight. And what is the difference between the *barma rabjung* and the *gesul* vows?

Rinpoche: The real difference between the *barma rabjung* vows and the *getsul* vows is you have not fully committed yourself to the vows in the *barma rabjung*. In a sense you are really examining and testing yourself to see whether you are able to commit yourself fully. Although you have not officially committed yourself, you have made up your mind that you don't want to be a householder, so you are practicing all the commitments without having received the official ordained commitments. In the *barma rabjung* there are five basic vows. The other vows haven't yet been taken yet officially, it is considered as mental training, or a test for yourself. Therefore there is no transgression if the additional vows are broken.

However, in the *getsul* vows, one has actually taken the ten vows and if these are transgressed, it is quite severe. The ten vows are known as the four defeats and six confessions. Included in the ten vows are not drinking alcohol, not indulging in music and dancing, not wearing jewelry, not touching gold or wealth, and not taking meals after midday. In China and Tibet the vow of not eating after midday is not observed. This has been previously explained. Briefly, the Theravādins observe the precept of not eating after midday because they live strictly on the food they receive when they go into the town on their morning alms round and the afternoon is reserved for practicing. If Tibetans had to beg from house-to-house in the village both in the morning and the afternoon, there would be little time left for practice. So in Tibet and China, the tradition of begging was not developed.

The *getsul* vows are somehow incomplete without having practiced the *barma rabjung* vows which include the *genyen* prātimokṣha vows. The *barma rabjung* vows are a test of whether one is able to keep the vows for one's whole life, before one takes the *getsul* vows. But this does not mean that it is temporary like the *nyen ne* vow, the one day fasting vow which is completed after one day. When you have found that you are actually able to keep all the vows, they are not given up. So in this sense they are not temporary.

Question: Rinpoche, I'm confused about the distinction between a vow and merely having an aspiration. There are many lay practitioners in our saṅgha who have accepted their meditation practice together with all the trainings as a basic part of their lives. Many of us feel that these aspirations are permanent and if we are not living up to those aspirations, we try to correct that problem.

Rinpoche: The word "vow" may not convey the full meaning of the Tibetan word *dom pa.* The English language does not seem to have a term strong enough to communicate the meaning of *dom pa.* The ten unwholesome actions are not regarded as an actual vow because if something is not within one's control, one cannot make a commitment or take an oath not to do it. For example, promising not to steal can be regarded as a vow because one can say, "I will never steal" in front of one's guru or in front of the shrine of an enlightened being. Stealing is a physical activity that is within one's control. If the thought of stealing occurs, one can remember having promised one's guru or the buddhas not to steal. One cannot, however, promise not to have certain thoughts. For example, we cannot promise, taking the guru as witness, that we will never have any envious thoughts. The moment we see something very attractive, envious thoughts occur in the mind so rapidly that there is no control over them. Because there is no control over them we cannot take the vow. But we have to understand that when we do not take a vow, that does not mean that we are not practicing to get rid of mental afflictions. As we develop samādhi, we gradually develop control over our mind and when we have control over our mind, then we can really eliminate envious feelings, harsh thoughts, and so on. If that is not the case, we cannot promise to have no envious thoughts and therefore the vow is not given to the student by the teacher.

Question: I wonder if Rinpoche would comment on how the precepts are kept and how they are broken, not by mind alone but on the level of accomplishment.

Rinpoche: We misunderstand the nature of the precepts if we do not separate the precept itself from the mental training or practice involved in it. For example, in the mental training of not developing any thought intended to deceive others, we become familiar with the virtue of the absence of even the thought of telling a lie. This training is very wholesome, but it is not the precept. The precept itself is the action of lying.

Four factors must be present for completely breaking the precept. First, there must be the object, the individual whom you want to deceive. This individual must be capable of understanding your lie. If it's an animal, no matter what words you use, it will not understand, so your deception will not be fulfilled. Second, is the intention of wanting to deceive that particular person or recipient. Third, is actualizing your intention by the actual words. Fourth, is the finalizing of the action so the individual actually hears your words. So if the recipient hears your deceptive words, whether or not he is actually deceived by them, you have broken the precept because you had the intention to deceive; the recipient was present, and you actualized your deceptive thought. But if you are staying alone under a tree in the jungle and tell yourself a lie, you are not breaking the vow because you are alone, there is no one who hears you. The four factors must be present for completely breaking the precept. Therefore the mental awareness training is different from taking the precepts.

Chapter 11

The Vows of the Bodhisattva

We have already talked about the prātimokṣha vow, which is the "outer" vow, because it deals with the disciplines of body and speech. Today we will deal with the inner vow, the bodhisattva vow, called "inner" because it concerns the discipline of mind. The prātimokṣha vow of the śhrāvaka is easy to preserve, because it is concerned with our outer behavior of body and speech which we can control by committing ourself to do such and such a thing physically or verbally. The outer discipline is a simple method of maintaining our conduct, and if it is transgressed, it cannot be renewed. The great teachers of the past compared the outer discipline to a clay pot which is hard and firm, but if dropped and broken, cannot be repaired. On the other hand, the inner bodhisattva vow is more difficult to keep because it deals with the mind which is constantly changing with thoughts which arise instantly and without choice. Therefore the bodhisattva vow is easily broken. The inner bodhisattva vow is compared to a vase made of pure gold which can become dented and deformed with the slightest knock but also can be repaired easily to its original condition.

The inner bodhisattva vow is concerned with the development of bodhichitta, enlightened mind which is accompanied by pure motivation. In Tibet the vows of prātimokṣha were considered to be very important. Since the outer discipline was mainly concerned with benefiting oneself, it was considered to be more effective to include the inner bodhisattva vow so that others would be benefited as well. For that reason Tibetan Buddhism did not pay detailed attention to all of the 252 vows of a fully ordained monk. Although the prātimokṣha vow is the foundation for all the other vows, to be fruitful, the inner bodhisattva vow is required. Likewise, one cannot commit oneself to the vajrayāna vows without having practiced the inner bodhisattva vows. So, the bodhisattva vows are regarded as very crucial and important because they act as a channel for both the prātimokṣha and the mahāyāna vows.

The bodhisattva vows are taken with the attitude of developing bodhichitta. One does not take the vows with the notion that one has perfected bodhichitta and from the moment of taken the vows, one will never break them. Because one's mind is constantly changing, one instead takes the bodhisattva vows with the aim of perfecting bodhichitta and as one goes along the path, one rejoices on learning that one is able to maintain the attitude of a bodhisattva and tries to develop that attitude further. The bodhisattva vows are traditionally renewed as often as one wants. Just as the more coats of paint you apply to a white-washed *stūpa,* the more strongly the paint stays on it.

There are three types of discipline to develop the bodhisattva vow. The first is abandoning and cutting through unwholesome and harmful actions, the second is gathering or accumulating virtuous and helpful dharmas, and the third one is benefiting sentient beings.

The Buddha turned the wheel of the dharma three times. In the first turning, he taught the hīnayāna and in the second turning he taught the mahāyāna which is concerned with emptiness (Skt. *śhūnyatā*). Later the great master Nāgārjuna clarified the hidden meanings of the Buddha's teachings [in commentaries on the Prajñāpāramitā literature]. Thinking that some of the teachings of the Buddha were extremely complicated and hard for ordinary people to understand, he wrote a very concise version of the teachings which were simple to understand. The commentaries by Nāgārjuna are known the "*transmission of the profound view.*" Then later, the great master Asaṅga, having the same intention of clarifying the hidden words of the Buddha, also condensed the more difficult teachings so that ordinary people could comprehend them. This became known as the "*transmission of vast conduct*," which deals with emptiness, but also with the bodhisattva levels and the path of enlightenment. Although these two transmissions of Asaṅga and Nāgārjuna differ slightly, they are concerned with transforming disturbing emotions or kleśhas into something positive by learning to develop a pure attitude of bodhichitta, loving-kindness, and compassion..

To illustrate such transformation there is one of the previous incarnations of Buddha who was born as the bodhisattva Captain Courage (Tib. *jed pon ying tos chan*). He went to sea in a big ship with five hundred merchants in search of jewels. On that ship was a wicked man who wanted to destroy the five hundred merchants by making a hole in the ship so that it would sink and all would be drowned. Knowing his evil thought, the bodhisattva killed him by hitting him on the head with an ax. Now we know that killing in general is not a positive action at all, but in this case the killing was based on the attitude of bodhichitta to save the lives of 500 people and to prevent the wicked man from accumulating a lot of negative karma. Therefore the action contributed to accumulation of positive karma not to the accumulation of negative karma.

So with the first type of the bodhisattva vow, one abandons or cuts through unwholesome or negative actions, even though such action might appear to be negative outwardly. If one is able to inwardly maintain a pure mind of love and compassion of bodhichitta, then one is able to transform negative conduct into positive action.

With the second type of bodhisattva vow, one accumulates virtuous dharmas by practicing the six pāramitās. There is a difference between the ordinary practice and the transcendental practice of the six perfections (Skt. *pāramitās*). One can practice all six of these perfections without the purity of heart of bodhichitta, which would be the ordinary practice rather than the transcendental practice. By tuning oneself into the transcendental mode of practicing the perfections, by having the pure attitude of bodhichitta, one develops wisdom—prajñā and jñāna. So whether one is practicing the discipline of cutting through all harmful actions or the discipline of accumulating wholesome dharmas, bodhichitta is absolutely essential. If bodhichitta is absent, trying to avoid negative actions is not the discipline of cutting through all harmful actions. Similarly, practicing generosity without cultivating bodhichitta is just ordinary giving, not the bodhisattva accumulation of wholesome dharmas.

The third type is the skillful means of benefiting others is known as "the four ways of magnetizing sentient beings." The first of these is giving what is needed. Of course whatever is given, it is a very generous act of a pure heart. Specifically, one tries to analyze intellectually what is most beneficial for each and every individual, and tries to provide that according to their needs. But here one must also learn not to become separated from bodhichitta. Not only does one please the other at that particular moment by providing what he or she needs, but also, by developing bodhichitta and praying, one applies the skillful means that can gradually turn the mind toward the dharma. By giving what is needed, one not only frees the individual temporarily from the pain of not having what is needed, but also one liberates them ultimately by providing the dharma.

The second way of magnetizing is by uttering pleasant words. With the development of bodhichitta, one pleases others by speaking in a very genuine, simple way that is helpful and soothing. In this regard, it is of utmost importance not to be deceptive or too intellectual.

The third way of magnetizing is known as acting in accordance with the world. To benefit sentient beings, one tries to provide them with the dharma that is at the level of the individual's capacity to understand. For a beginner it is not beneficial to give them high teachings which they may not comprehend. Therefore one should give the beginner the simplest form of teachings. As the person progresses, one should not provide them with the same level of teachings lest they become bored, but give more advanced teachings to advanced students, and extremely advanced teaching to those have the intellectual capacity to understand. It is the duty of the dharma teacher to adjust the teachings to the individual's ability which is known as acting in accordance with the world. The example is that a mother does not give her infant solid food which the child cannot eat, but gives it milk. But as the child grows, she gives it food that is more and more solid, and when the child is older she gives it solid food, not milk.

The fourth way of magnetizing is called acting in accordance with the disciple or "practice what you teach." Whatever one teaches the student, one must show that one practices or has practiced that same teaching. In this way the mind of the student becomes inspired. In the Tibetan tradition, leprosy is believed to be caused by the curse of the nāgas, and so to avoid catching leprosy, people practiced the garuḍa sadhāna and mantra. If you say that you practice the garuḍa sadhāna and mantra but you have leprosy, it means you have not been practicing it properly. So one must really prove that one is practicing whatever teachings that one is providing.

To benefit sentient beings mindfulness (Tib. *dren pa*), awareness (Tib. *she zhin pa*) and alertness (Tib. *bag yod pa*) are further means of making one's actions beneficial. Mindfulness means that when one is trying to benefit others, one must be mindful that one is acting in accordance with bodhichitta. Awareness means that one examines oneself again and again, as many times as is possible, to see how strongly one is rooted in bodhichitta. Alertness means that one is very careful and cautious not to go against bodhichitta. By means of these three, one becomes very skillful in actually providing whatever is necessary to benefit sentient beings.

Questions

Question: Rinpoche, in regard to giving other people what they need, sometimes it seems that they need something that they don't want. It's difficult to be sure that what you're actually giving them is beneficial and does not come from some problem of your own that you have with the other person. Would you please say more about how we can give people what they need without causing harm at the same time?

Rinpoche: In giving what others need, we must not give blindly. From our part, we must not be confused ourselves and we must be quite clear when we are giving. Our first responsibility in performing generosity is to have a clear mind. With a clear mind we can carefully analyze what the individual is asking for or needs, and whether what we are providing is beneficial or not. As explained earlier, the purpose of giving here is to please the outer individual's mind, that he or she can turn to the dharma. In that sense, generosity does not mean giving a great amount of things, but even a simple thing, a simple gesture, may be sufficient to please the other. However, in case of an extremely stubborn, difficult person whom you don't fully know what they really need, it is not proper to perform generosity because, in your own mind, the reason for giving is not clear. So, if you have any doubt, it is better not to do anything,

Question: Rinpoche, we seem to have the habit that we want to cut one another's trips. Is it possible to do this skillfully without being critical?

Rinpoche: It is our responsibility to examine ourselves carefully to see that our being critical of somebody is not for our own personal benefit or personal gain. We must examine our own mind to see that our main goal is to benefit the other individual, that our altruistic motive is concentrated on helping that person. Then we have to see whether being critical would be beneficial to the other person, to the whole community in the long run, or whether being critical would develop more anger or hatred between us and the other person, or among the saṅgha. Having examined this carefully, if we see that it wouldn't cause resentment or hatred and there would be no harm to the community and that it is a proper thing to do, then we must approach this person, not in a harsh way, but very gently, and explain what we think is proper.

Question: Trungpa Rinpoche taught us about idiot compassion. He encouraged us to examine our behavior, our motives, our minds, as to how we help others. Would Rinpoche please comment on that?

Rinpoche: Not only is there idiot compassion, but there is idiot loving kindness, idiot generosity, and idiot patience. Gampopa in *The Jewel Ornament of Liberation* explains clearly that giving with a confused mind is idiot generosity and that one must abandon this and learn to practice pure generosity. In the case of compassion, sometimes the person who is receiving the compassionate gesture may not appreciate it and react negatively. That means that one has not examined oneself properly before providing the gesture. Further, one should examine whether one's compassionate action may be beneficial to one individual, but harmful to somebody else. Therefore it is the practitioner's responsibility to examine very carefully to see that the compassion being provided is of tremendous benefit to that person and is not harmful to anyone. That is compassion without confusion.

Question: Would you please present the Shentong view of bodhichitta?

Rinpoche: The present talk has given a general explanation of the importance of developing and practicing bodhichitta. But we must understand the level which we are actually at. It has been argued that Buddhism claims to benefit others but apparently does not do so, whereas other religions, such as Christianity, actually provide alms and charity and material support to the needy. They claim that Buddhists simply lock themselves up in solitary retreat, and how could this be of benefit to others? This argument has existed for a long time. The idea of bodhichitta is that we develop a very pure kind heart. But at present our compassion and wisdom is not sufficient and we must train ourselves. Not having sufficient wisdom and compassion, when we try to provide something for someone that we think would be of benefit, later on we regret that we have given it because it was harmful rather than helping someone. This is because we do not have enough wisdom to foresee the future of our actions. Therefore, in the beginning we must develop our love, wisdom, and compassion by practicing meditation. When we have developed sufficiently, we do not need to force ourselves to develop this kind of pure attitude, because it becomes quite effortless.

Some people are discouraged and do not have faith in this buddha nature. They think: "I cannot attain enlightenment. I do not have that capacity." With that negative attitude, they ignore their own potential to become enlightened and belittle themselves. Not only that, they become critical of Buddhahood and the whole idea of enlightenment. This is the result of not knowing that every sentient being has within ourselves. The Shentong view teaches that every living being has buddha nature and buddha qualities. Therefore each of us can achieve Buddhahood if we exert ourselves. There is no need to belittle ourselves and to put ourselves down. Therefore the Shentong view is very inspiring to those who have little knowledge of the buddha qualities within themselves.

Question: Does the discovery of emptiness brings about genuine compassion?

Rinpoche: It's true that "Emptiness is the essence of compassion." The reason for this is that through ignorance or confusion, we project something that does not exist: saṃsāra. Having projected saṃsāra, we experience happiness and sadness and suffering. Sometimes, when we are temporarily happy and comfortable, we fear that the happiness will cease. So there is no complete happiness in the confused state of saṃsāra. Still others experience misery and very deep suffering in saṃsāra. So the nature of saṃsāra itself is suffering. When we have realized emptiness (Skt. śhūnyatā), there is no more suffering, no fear that the happiness will cease. Therefore by realizing emptiness we will become very compassionate to those who are still confused and worried that their happiness will end. The analogy of this is a person who has a nightmare of being chased by fierce wild animals. Because the dream, the confused state of mind, is so real to him, the person sleeping actually experiences pain and suffering. But suppose there is a clairvoyant person who sees that this person is having a nightmare and that person is terrified. The clairvoyant person would have compassion for this person who is suffering and go to this sleeping individual and wake him up out of his confused state of dreams saying, "There's nothing to be frightened of, you are just dreaming." The clairvoyant person is like someone who has realized emptiness and the person who is dreaming is like a person trapped in saṃsāra.

Chapter 12

The Vows of the Vajrayāna

There are four major schools of Buddhism in Tibet: the Sākyapa, Nyingmapa, Kagyupa, and Gelugpa. They all practice the vajrayāna. Tibetan Buddhism, however, is an integration of all three vehicles: the outer vows of individual liberation, the inner bodhisattva vow of the development of bodhichitta, and the samaya vows of the vajrayāna. There are four main tantras in the vajrayāna: the kriyātantra, the caryātantra, the yogatantra, and the anuttarayogatantra. Of these four, yogatantra deals with inner and outer practice whereas anuttarayogatantra deals strictly with secret tantra. According to the tradition of the Nyingma school there are nine yānas or the śhrāvakayāna, pratyekabuddhayāna and bodhisatvayāna, which are known as the characteristic yānas. Then there are the kriyātantra, carayatantra, and yogatantra which are known as the three outer tantras; and finally the mahāyoga, the anuyoga, and atiyoga tantras are known as the three inner tantras. According to the system of the Kagyu school, the nine yānas consist of the śhrāvakayāna, pratyekbuddhayāna and mahāyāna which make up the sūtrayāna and the kriyātantra, carayatantra, and yogatantras are known as the outer tantras. The anuttarayogatantra is subdivided into the father tantra, the mother tantra, and the union tantra which makes nine tantras in all.

There are three aspects of a tantra: firstly skillful means and wisdom; secondly, the developing and accomplishing stages of meditation; and thirdly, the experiences of luminosity and emptiness. The father tantra emphasizes skillful means, the developing stage of meditation, and luminosity. The mother tantra emphasizes wisdom, the accomplishing stage of meditation, and emptiness. In the union tantra equally emphasizes both skillful means and wisdom. Since these are inseparable in this union tantra it is called in Tibetan *gnyis med* or literally "no twoness."

The teachings of mahāmudrā can be related to both the sūtrayāna and the tantrayāna. This goes back to Gampopa who in a previous incarnation was a student of śhākyamuni Buddha with the Tibetan name of Zlaöd Zhanu. After Buddha had taught the *Samādhiraja sūtra* to five hundred bodhisattvas, he asked, "Who will propagate clarify, and develop the *Samādhiraja sūtra* in the future dark age?" Zlaöd Zhanu stood up and vowed, "I will make clear the meaning of the *Samādhiraja sūtra* and develop it." When he had said this, the rest of the five hundred bodhisattvas rejoiced and vowed that they too would help to propagate the meaning of this sūtra. Then the Buddha blessed Zlaöd Zhanu placing his hand on his head and prophesied that in the future he would be reborn as a physician named Dagpo Lharje at Rohita in southern Tibet near the Brahmaputra River, a place with many forests and medicinal plants. In fulfillment of this prophecy Gampopa Dagpo Lharje, clarified the meaning of the *Samādhiraja* sūtra doing this not by giving teachings on the words of the *Samādhiraja*, but by propagating its meaning as the realization of meditation. Gampopa taught the mahāmudrā which deals strictly with the inner development of the mind in meditation which is the equivalent of spreading this sūtra.

Gampopa had received the sūtrayāna teaching through the line coming down from Atiśha. To explain the reason for Atiśha's visit to Tibet we must begin with the first transmission of the dharma to Tibet. Initially, in the first phase (in 9th century C. E.) Buddhism was adopted in a very pure form by Tibetans in a transmission free from impurities. But later, King Langdarma (ruled 901-906 C. E.) destroyed Buddhism in Tibet and for some time the country remained without the teachings. After Langdarma's death, when the Tibetan people tried to restore the buddhadharma again, but the teachings were not as orderly and pure as before. Therefore the two kings, Lha Yeshe Od and Lha Changchup Od, heard about the great scholar in India named Atīsha and invited him to Tibet to eliminate any impurities and faults and to provide correct and precise teachings to the people of Tibet. Atīsha (892-1055 C. E.) came and paid great attention to the sūtrayāna and in particular in taking of refuge and bodhichitta.

In his teachings on mahāmudrā Gampopa with his skillfulness, condensed the whole transmission of the five sūtrayānas of Atīśha into a very short meaningful and effective instructions for his students which he called "sūtrayāna mahāmudrā" and combined these with the transmission he had received from his guru Milarepa from the line of Shavaripa, Saraha, Maitripa, and Marpa.

Mahāmudrā teachings therefore cannot be said to belong to the sūtrayāna nor can it be said they belong strictly to tantrayāna. It is a transmission taken from the teachings of both sūtrayāna and the mantrayāna, so it is a combination of these two traditions. In the *Moonlight of Mahāmudrā* Takpo Tashi Namgyal explains that the mahāmudrā is a transmission that is neither sūtrayāna nor tantrayāna alone. So mahāmudrā can be practiced in either of two ways: either without dependence of skillful means of using prāṇa and nādī[7] and looking directly at the nature of the mind or by utilizing skillful means and relating with prāṇa and the nādī.

Since everything is mind, the emphasis of mahāmudrā is directed toward learning the nature of one's mind. For exam-

[7]Skillful means (Skt. *upaya*) are advanced yogic practices which deal with the subtle energies or "winds" (Skt. *prāṇa*, Tib. *lung*) of the body which flow through the subtle channels (Skt. *nādī*, Tib. *tsa*) of the body.

ple, the Madhyamaka teaches that the nature of mind is emptiness and primordial wisdom (Skt. *jñāna*). But to arrive at such an understanding one uses logical reasoning to understand the emptiness of all phenomena and the emptiness of self. The Madhyamaka school teaches a method for understanding emptiness using reasoning and intellectual means, but it is a very long process. Since one realizes the mind as the root of everything in mahāmudrā, one meditates directly on the mind in order to see its emptiness, without relating to the emptiness of phenomena.

Because of the importance of relating meditation to the inner mind and its emptiness, Trungpa Rinpoche introduced his students, at a certain stage, to ultimate knowledge or awareness, *ordinary mind* (Tib. *thamal gyi she pa)*. Having been given such powerful skillful means, we must learn how to apply it to whatever practice we may be doing, whether it be śhamatha, the preliminary ngondro practices, or the yidam practice of Vajrayoginī or Cakrasaṃvara. So it is of utmost importance to combine one's practice with ordinary mind. This ordinary mind has been introduced by Trungpa Rinpoche to many students and it is therefore very important that it must never be forgotten.

In this respect there is a humorous story about the eighth Karmapa, Mikyo Dorje. One day he became slightly upset with his student and told them in a critical way that no Kagyu student will attain enlightenment because they are like a balloon full of air. Although the balloon holds the air, it cannot attain enlightenment. What the Karmapa said has tremendous inner meaning. What he meant is that if people like ourselves practice prāṇa along with *thamal gyi shepa*, then we have the opportunity to experience enlightenment. However, if we forget about thamal gyi she pa and simply hold the air or prāṇa within ourselves, then we are like a balloon[8] and how could we possibly attain enlightenment? So I want to request all of you never to forget to include *thamal gyi she pa* in your practice whether it be śhamatha or the generation or completion stages of Vajrayoginī. Please do not neglect ordinary mind. Many students have not had the fortunate karma of having been introduced to ordinary mind. You who are students of Trungpa Rinpoche are very fortunate in having had this introduction.

Questions

Question: Rinpoche, you made the comment that mahāmudrā is neither sūtrayāna nor tantrayāna. Would you say more about that?

Rinpoche: The statement in Tashi Namgyal's book that mahāmudrā is neither sūtrayāna nor tantrayāna means that the mahāmudrā teachings are not entirely sūtrayāna teachings nor entirely tantrayāna teachings. Whatever is very profound and meaningful in the sūtrayāna has been taken out and put into mahāmudrā, and whatever is very profound and meaningful in the tantrayāna has been taken out and put into mahāmudrā. Therefore, in essence, the mahāmudrā is not exactly like the sūtrayāna teachings and not exactly like the tantrayāna teachings, but it is the essence of the entire dharma and is an integration of both.

But at the same time, it is not sūtrayāna because in the Madhyamika teachings of the sūtrayāna one is introduced to meditation by way of logic and the intellect. However, this intellectual method of the Madhyamika is not used in the mahāmudrā which is a method of directly looking straight at the mind. At the same time, it is not tantrayāna because in

[8]There is a practice of vase breathing in which one holds the breath for a very long time in the lower abdomen to allow the air to enter the central channel.

the tantrayāna the creation stage and the completion stage are applied and mahāmudrā does not involve these two stages. By the realization of mahāmudrā, one actually achieves the fruition of both sūtrayāna and tantrayāna simultaneously.

Question: Is the main reason that mahāmudrā is not tantrayāna because there is no generation or completion stage in mahāmudrā?

Rinpoche: Correct. However, we must understand that mahāmudrā can be related to the generating and completion stages of meditation as well, even though within the mahāmudrā teachings there is no generating or completion stage. When actually doing the developing stage, at the end of it, you can put yourself into mahāmudrā which would be an effective way of practicing mahāmudrā.

Question: It was said that one could experience mahāmudrā by looking directly at the nature of the mind without utilizing the inner yogas of breath and so on. Could you please say something about how these yogas are used and what are their benefits?

Rinpoche: Mahāmudrā, looking directly at the nature of mind, is the path of liberation. Meditation on prāṇa, nādīs, and tigles is the path of skillful means. If we integrate the meditation of looking directly into the nature of the mind and with the accompanying understanding of the nature of the mind with the prāṇa and the tigle, then what we realize on the path of liberation can be increased by virtue of the path of skillful means.

In the teachings of the ninth Karmapa, Wangchuk Dorje, in his *The Mahamudra: Eliminating the Darkness of Ignorance* or of Pema Karpo, there are no specific instructions on the generating stage such as how one should visualize the deity's color, shape, number of arms, and so forth. In the same teachings there are no specific instructions on the subtle airs or channels or how one should breathe in and out in the completion stage. That is why it is said that there is no generating or completion stage in mahāmudrā. What actually is taught, particularly in Pema Karpo's teachings, are examples of how to look directly at the nature of mind. One example of this is from Saraha who discusses this process in terms of spinning a thread. When you spin a thread, it must not be spun too tight or too loose. Another example is in Wangchuk Dorje's teaching, you must recognize the mind at rest and become aware of the difference between the resting mind and the moving mind when thoughts are arising. So those are the methods taught by Wangchuk Dorje and Pema Karpo that introduce the nature of mind rather than the visualization of the deity in the generating stage.

Question: In the *Moonlight of Mahāmudrā,* Tashi Namgyal says that we should not combine the direct realization of enlightened mind and the path of the nādīs and prāṇa. Would you please comment on that?

Rinpoche: When you are being taught mahāmudrā, direct realization of mind and the practice of bindu and nādī should not be combined. However, when you are practicing the Six Yogas of Nāropa they are combined. So there is no problem in combining the path of skillful means or the exercises of Wangchuk Dorje with the practice of the yidam.

Question: How is mahāmudrā included in the mahāyāna practices such as sending and taking practice (Tib. *tonglen*)?

Rinpoche: The essential nature of the mind is free from all obscurations. One must develop familiarity with that nature. Having become familiar with that, one then must maintain that awareness all the time. Whether one is doing the generating stage of meditation or whether one is practicing tonglen, one must maintain that awareness of the nature of the mind. That's very important.

Chapter 13

The Samaya Vow

Previously, we discussed the highest anuttarayoga tantra and its two divisions, the father and mother tantras. Now we will discuss the essence of the vajrayāna practice which is one's connection with one's root guru.

The guru is the most important part in one's life, in the vajrayāna teachings he is known as the origin of all blessings. Whether one is able to receive the blessings or develop powers (Skt. *siddhis)* depends on one's relationship with the guru.

Some schools of Buddhism claim that Tibetan Buddhism holds the guru higher than the Buddha and this is wrong because the śhākyamuni Buddha is the origin of all the teachings. Although it is true the guru is very important in Tibetan Buddhism, the guru is not regarded as being higher than the Buddha. The Buddha did take birth in our human world and turned the wheel of dharma, but it is only from the guru that we can receive the blessings and therefore, in our present circumstances, the guru plays the most important role.

The body of the Buddha possesses inconceivable qualities, the speech of the Buddha possesses inconceivable qualities, and the mind of the Buddha possesses inconceivable qualities. There is a large amount of time separating us from the Buddha because we did not have the good fortune of being born during the time of śhākyamuni Buddha. So the only way we can come to know the inconceivable qualities of the Buddha's body, speech, and mind is through the kindness of the guru who holds the unbroken transmission from the Buddha and who shows us that such inconceivable qualities do exist. Without the guru we would have no means of receiving the teachings, therefore we should have the utmost gratitude to the guru.

There are two kinds of gurus: the root guru and the transmission guru. The transmission guru includes all those who hold the unbroken transmission up to the present time. The root guru, in addition to holding the unbroken transmission, is the particular guru to whom we are very strongly connected in this lifetime and to whom we are very open. For this reason it is said that the root guru is the embodiment of the essence of all the buddhas of the ten directions, of the thousand kalpas, and of the three times. The ten directions means "in all directions," the thousand kalpas means "all the eons of time," and the three times mean "past, present, and future." The intention of all the buddhas is to benefit all sentient beings. Since it is the root guru who makes the compassion of all the buddhas available to us, he or she is said to be the embodiment of all the buddhas.

The purpose of the dharma is to liberate us from the pain and misery of saṃsāra. It is the root guru who gives us the technique for liberation from suffering and who makes the dharma available to us. Therefore the root guru is also said to be the embodiment of all the dharma. The degree to which the strength of the dharma develops in us depends on our confidence and trust in the guru. If our trust in the guru is very strong, infallible, then the fruition of our dharma practice will develop.

The saṅgha is a guide along the path, spiritual friends that helps us to eliminate obstacles and hindrances and provides us with all the necessities for practice. Whenever we become discouraged, the saṅgha provides encouragement to practice. Because the guru is the spiritual friend who grants us all of these and guides us very precisely along the path, the guru is said to be the embodiment of all the saṅghas. So the guru can be said to embody the three jewels—the Buddha, the Dharma, and the Saṅgha.

Although there are many commitments in the vajrayāna, it is said that if our relationship with the root guru is pure and we maintain the samayas of the body, speech and mind of the root guru, then we are preserving the purity of all the vajrayāna samayas.

The first samaya is of the body of the guru. We may wonder that since we receive instructions from the guru, that the speech of the guru would be most important. However, devotion to the body of the guru leads you to have devotion to the speech of the guru and as a result, weenjoy practicing what the guru has taught. If, on the contrary, we feel aggression or pride or any of the disturbing emotions when we see the physical form of the guru, that act constitutes breaking the samaya of the body of the guru. The extreme of breaking the samaya of body would be to become so angry at the guru that we actually strike the guru.

The second samaya is the samaya of the speech of the guru. Having devotion to the guru's speech, we can then apply the teachings of the guru to ourselves. Also we must always be sure that we do not regard the guru's speech to be the same as ordinary people's speech. If we forget the preciousness of the guru's speech because we lack respect and devotion for the guru's speech, then there will be no inspiration and we will be unable to practice what the guru has taught. Therefore we must maintain love, care, and devotion to the speech of the guru.

We also should not disregard or pass judgment on any of the guru's teachings accepting only what we consider of interest to ourselves. The Buddha offered the dharma to all beings in this world. His teachings were applicable to each and everyone's needs and they contained the remedy for attachment, aggression, and ignorance. However, as ordinary beings, we are not sufficiently advanced to be able to choose the remedy for our own neurosis. The guru is the one who knows what weaknesses we have to work on and the guru makes the appropriate hīnayāna, mahāyāna, and vajrayāna disciplines available to us. Thus, regardless of what vehicle the guru may teach, we must appreciate and treasure every word.

The third samaya of the mind of the guru is subdivided into two categories. The first is accomplishing the intention of the guru. Whatever transmissions we have received from the guru, we must follow and appreciate them. The reason the guru has handed us the teachings is for us to practice them. For this we must first learn about all the profound aspects of this teaching and then we should practice them. But practicing them is not the final stage. We should practice them in such a diligent way that through our exertion and determination, we experience some realization. Until that happens, we really have to keep working to fulfill the intention of the guru.

The second category of samaya of the guru's mind consists of supporting and protecting the guru's activity. To understand the guru's activity, we must fully comprehend that the intention of the guru is to make the teachings available so he or she can liberate all sentient beings. Therefore we have the responsibility to carry out the activity of the guru of making the teachings available to students both now and as long as saṃsāra exists so that future students can liberate others. To this end we must develop courage to assist the guru in accomplishing these intentions and to further the guru's activities of pacifying, enriching, magnetizing, and destroying.

This has been a brief explanation of the samayas of the guru's body, speech, and mind. The important point is that if the samayas are maintained purely, then fruition of Buddhahood is possible. But if we lack this purity, then fruition is very difficult to attain. These then are the three vows, the *dom sum* or the outer prātimokṣha vow, the inner bodhisattva vow, and the secret mantrayāna or vajrayāna vow. In each monastery the teacher applies these vows differently according to what seems appropriate for the particular students. However, the purpose of all three vows is the same: to pacify and eliminate the kleśhas based on training the mind. As Milarepa sang in one of his dohās: "I don't care about vinaya or sūtrayāna. All that I care about is to tame this wild mind."

Questions

Question: Rinpoche, would you please explain the root guru and transmission guru.

Rinpoche: We must he very grateful to our root guru who makes the transmission of the dharma available to us. We must also be greatful to the transmission gurus who were our guru's teacher and then his own root guru who gave him the unbroken transmission would be the transmission gurus. In the Kagyu tradition there are many transmission gurus beginning with Vajradarma then Tilopa, Nāropa, Marpa, Milarepa, Gampopa, and so on. The transmission gurus have handed down the transmission in an uninterrupted way from the time of śhākyamuni Buddha until today.

Question: When discussing the first aspect of the samaya of the guru's mind, you spoke about the need first to understand the profound meaning, secondly, to apply the practice to oneself, and thirdly, to develop some realization. Would Rinpoche please say more about what that means.

Rinpoche: Having thoroughly studied and understood the profound meaning of the transmission, you apply the teaching to yourself through the practice. As you practice, you should not try to calculate your achievement by the number of mantras you have done or by how long you have practiced. You should just simply practice until there is some realization. For example, one of my former translators said, "There is no real power in dharma practice. I have done the ngondro practices and I have completed the Vajrapāṇi practice, yet nothing has happened." That was a very discouraging comment. We should not dwell on numbers or time, but simply practice until we gain some experience of realization.

Question: Rinpoche, when one is dreaming and one is aware that one is dreaming, what should one do?

Rinpoche: When you know within your dream that you are dreaming, then it is quite helpful if you can practice that you want to go to the pure realm of the Buddha or that you want to go to meet your guru or try to visualize the particular yidam that you are familiar with. However, you should not force yourself to do too much in your dream.

Question: Would Rinpoche say something about samaya to the absolute guru, especially now that the relative guru for us has passed away.

Rinpoche: The mind of the guru is completely realized, the dharmadhātu, therefore there is no difference between the absolute and the relative guru. Although the guru has departed physically, his compassionate attitude, his buddha activity, the transmissions have been left with us. He left us with the trust that we will carry them on to future generations. Therefore if we complete the practices and make them available to others; that is the fulfillment of the samayas of the body, speech, and mind of the guru.

Question: Would you please say something about the Thrangu lineage and about yourself.[9]

Rinpoche: What you see is it. [Laughter] I have no special qualities nor have I any diligence in dharma practice. Several times I wondered how I came to be recognized as Thrangu Rinpoche. I have no inner realization of mind. When we read about the previous Thrangu Rinpoches, their activities and realization were inconceivable, but I myself do not possess even a fraction of their realization. When I was very young, I asked my Abbot "I have no inner qualities. Why did His Holiness Karmapa recognize me as Thrangu Rinpoche? Will these qualities develop when I get older?" My khenpo was quite discouraging. He said, "If you don't have any inner qualities now, they won't grow later." Eventually, I came to understand why His Holiness recognized me as Thrangu Rinpoche. If he had not done so, I would be wandering around, doing business, and be very much attached to saṃsāric things. To prevent me from becoming materialistic and attached to worldly activities, His Holiness, by recognizing me as a tulku, gave me the opportunity to study and practice.

However, having said that, you might wonder whether the teachings you received are reliable. Though I have no inner personal realization I spent much time hearing, contemplating, and meditating on the teachings so that the transmission of the buddhadharma that I am giving to you is being given exactly as it was in the past, without any exaggeration. You need not have any doubts about the teachings.

Rinpoche: In closing, I would like to make few comments which may possibly help you in the future so that your devotion and trust will not be shaken. Some university professors, who themselves are not practitioners, say that the Tibetan commentaries have no value and that you should relate directly to the original teachings of the Buddha. This may seem to be correct in that what is important to us is the very teachings of the Buddha. But as we have already discussed, the inner meaning of the Buddha's teachings are sometimes hidden, and because of the vastness of the teachings, they are sometimes scattered. The benefit of the Tibetan commentaries is that they make the inner hidden meanings available and gather together the scattered meanings. Therefore studying the commentaries of Tibetan teachers is not contradictory to studying the teachings of the Buddha himself.

Chapter 14

This is my Monastery

An address given by the Venerable Thrangu Rinpoche to the monastic saṅgha at Gampo Abbey in October, 1989.

In general, monks and nuns are not the same as a family because a "regular" lay family comes together because of desire and attachment and because in a family one gives up one's own individual freedom so one no longer has individual choice. In order to get away from the situation of desire and attachment, and to gain one's freedom again, one becomes ordained as a monk or nun.

But having become ordained we still needs within our newly gained freedom something which encourages one to practice and facilitates dealing with obstacles, like sickness, disease, old age and death, which are so difficult to deal with if one is completely on our own. Therefore the Buddha established the saṅgha as a group of people who have basically given up any attachment and desire, yet live within a group in order to deal more easily with difficulties and to encourage general perseverance and diligence. If there is no one living with us to remind us about our position, then we might easily do whatever we want and then maybe nothing would come out of our commitment and aspiration. In other words, after our initial choice for independence or freedom it is possible that there could actually be too much independence or freedom and we could just get lost in our own independence and freedom. Just like a wild animal we could think: "I am so happy No one can tell me what to do. There's nobody I have to answer to. I have no responsibilities and nothing to do. I can drink, smoke dope as much as I want and no one says anything. All I have to worry about is my own happiness, independence, and freedom." That is not what's meant by giving up family life.

The tradition of relying on one another, of practicing within a group, was developed by the Buddha. In this way the discipline of the monks and nuns was very controlled and their practice improved. There are many reasons why a monastic setting is good. In Tibet monks and nuns who are living in a monastery, have a great sense of identification with that monastery. If a monk or nun for some reason has to leave the monastery there's always the thought "I'm a resident of this monastery and I'll definitely come back and live here. I am of this monastery." If one is mindful and aware of one's adherence to one's monastery, one develops very conscientious behavior and activity. Therefore this sense of identification has great benefit. Generally the Buddha taught the dharma by way of training in discipline, meditation, and wisdom (Skt. *śhīla*, *samādhi*, and *prajñā*). By identifying oneself with a group at the monastery and thinking, "I am of this monastery, a place where training in śhīla, samādhi and prajñā are done" enables these three trainings become a part of oneself. One is constantly aware of them and so one doesn't forget them. One thinks, "This is what is being learned in my monastery. These are my friends, the saṅgha, who are all practicing the dharma." You carry this notion with you wherever you go, whether inside or outside the monastery. If you don't have this sense of identification with the group and the whole support system of the monastery and just wander around without any sense of belonging or bearing of where you are, you could easily forget these teachings and the training you have undergone.

In regards to discipline and moral conduct there is an agreement that everyone keeps the same discipline in a monastery. Therefore it is easy to keep discipline with "They all keep it, so I'm going to keep it too" or "I'm keeping fifteen precepts so they should keep them too."

If you leave the monastery and spend a lot of time with people with a different moral conduct, then after a while you will start to think, "All these people are doing something else. They are not keeping my kind of discipline and moral conduct. Why am I doing it? Why am I the only one who needs to do this? Why do I have to wear these clothes, nobody else is wearing these clothes?" So you slowly forget why you were even supposed to do it. For example, if you were to go into a bar where everyone is drinking except yourself, and you would just sit there and do nothing, after a while you would start thinking, "What kind of weird person am I that I am not joining in on these activities?" If you stay in a monastery you wouldn't have such difficulties. Nobody is drinking and everybody is keeping the same moral code. Therefore in a monastery you do not feel strange at all, but in harmony with everybody. You can easily remember keep the discipline and easily remember that there are real reasons and great benefits from doing so. It makes the whole life easier, more peaceful, and less complicated. In this way you don't waste your life. It is important for monks and nuns to remember the need and the necessity of discipline.

I go to Europe very often and in the past I have ordained many monks and nuns there. Every year I ordain a lot, but when I come back the next year, there are no monks and nuns. Then I ordain more monks and nuns, but again when I come back, no monks, no nuns. Therefore when people ask me now for ordination I say, "No. You probably won't be able to keep it." But then they say, "Oh, I really want to become a monk or nun. I'm definitely going to keep this ordination." So I give it, but when I come back the next year, no monk, no nun. Sometimes I get letters four or five months later saying, "I am sorry I just couldn't keep it. I'm not a monk any more." Sometimes it even lasts a year. So I ask them, "Why? What's the matter? Why can't you keep your ordination?"

Most of them say, "In the West it is impossible. Nobody can keep the vows."

Well, I don't think this is really true because there is a long monastic tradition in the West, the Catholic tradition. So I don't think that is the reason why people can't keep the ordination, especially as there is not much of a difference between a Buddhist monk and nun and a Christian monk and nun.

So what is the cause? I think it is because there are no Buddhist monasteries in the West. Therefore, years ago, I suggested that an organization called the International Kagyu Saṅgha Association be started. This was done with the hope that the Association would eventually be able to establish a monastery. I think that the establishment of a monastery is crucial for the development of Western monks and nuns. Once there is a monastery, then the monks and nuns can stay in it and manage to keep their vows for more than two or three months. They might even keep the vows for years.

Well, so far I was not able to establish this monastery as I was hoping to, but at least there's Gampo Abbey, which through the kindness of Trungpa Rinpoche has come about. So I think, because of this good luck of there being an Abbey, a monastery, that you monks and nuns will last longer than a few months.

So, for monks and nuns, monasteries are very, very important. You should think, "This is my monastery." And if you think in this way obstacles will never come up.

Glossary of Terms

Abhidharma (Tib. *chö ngön pa*) The Buddhist teachings are often divided into the Tripiṭaka: the sūtras (teachings of the Buddha), the vinaya (teachings on conduct), and the abhidharma which are the analysis of phenomena that exist primarily as a commentarial tradition to the Buddhist teachings. There is not, in fact, an abhidharma section within the Tibetan collection of the Buddhist teachings.

Akṣobhya (Tib. *mi bskyod pa*) The sambhogakāya buddha of the vajra family.

Amitābha One of the five buddha family deities known as "buddha of boundless light" Usually depicted as red.

Amoghasiddhi One of the five buddha families and means "all-accomplishing one." Usually depicted as green.

anuttara yoga tantra (Tib. *nal jor la na me pay jū*) There are four levels of the vajrayāna and annutara tantra is the highest of these. It contains the Guhyasamāja, the Chakrasaṃvara, the Hevajra, and the Kalāchakra tantras.

arhat (Tib. *dra chom pa*) Accomplished hīnayāna practitioners who have eliminated the kleśa obscurations. They are the fully realized śrāvakas and pratyekabuddhas.

Asaṅga (Tib. *thok me)* A fourth century Indian philosopher who founded the Chittamātra or Yogacara school and wrote the five works of Maitreya which are important mahāyāna works. Also brother of Vasubhandu.

Atiśa (982-1055 C. E.) Was a Buddhist scholar at Vikramaśilā University in India and came to Tibet at the invitation of the King to overcome the damage done by Langdarma. He helped found the Kadam tradition.

bhikṣhu (Tib. *ge long*) A fully ordained monk.

bindu (Tib. *tigle*) Vital essence drops or spheres of psychic energy which are often visualized in vajrayāna practices.

bodhicitta (Tib. *chang chup chi sem*) Literally, the mind of enlightenment. There are two kinds of bodhicitta: absolute bodhicitta, which is completely awakened mind that sees the emptiness of phenomena, and relative bodhicitta which is the aspiration to practice the six pāramitās and free all beings from the suffering of saṃsāra.

bodhisattva (Tib. *chang chup sem pa*) Literally, one who exhibits the mind of enlightenment. Also an individual who has committed him or herself to the mahāyāna path of compassion and the practice of the six pāramitās to achieve Buddhahood to free all beings from saṃsāra.

bodhisattva levels (Skt. *bhūmi,* Tib. *sa*) The levels or stages a bodhisattva goes through to reach enlightenment. These consist of ten levels in the sūtra tradition and thirteen in the tantra tradition.

bodhisattva vow A vow in which one promises to practice in order to bring all other sentient beings to Buddhahood.

buddha nature (Skt. *tathāgatagarbha,* Tib. *de shin shek pay nying po*) The original nature present in all beings which when realized leads to enlightenment. It is often called the essence of Buddhahood or enlightened essence.

buddhadharma The teachings of the Buddha.

Cakrasaṃvara (Tib. *korlo dompa*) A meditational deity which belongs to the annuttara tantra set of teachings.

Caryātantra The second of the four tantras empasizing meditation and external rituals.

compassion (Skt. *karuṇā,* Tib. *nying je*) In Buddhist terms this is the desire for liberation of all sentient beings regardless of who they are. This feeling can only be developed with extensive meditation and understanding of the Buddhist path.

completion stage (Tib. *dzo rim)* In the vajrayāna there are two stages of meditation: the development and the completion stage. The completion stage is a method of trantric meditation in which one attains bliss, clarity, and nonthought by means of the subtle channels and energies within the body.

creation stage (Skt. *utpattikrama*, Tib. *che rim*) In the vajrayāna there are two stages of meditation: the development and the completion stage. This is a method of tantric meditation which involves visualization and contemplating deities for the purpose of realizing the purity of all phenomena. In this stage visualization of the deity is established and maintained.

dharma (Tib. *chö*) This has two main meanings: Any truth such as the sky is blue and secondly, as used in this text, the teachings of ?also called buddhadharma).

dharmadhātu (Tib. *chö ying*) The all-encompassing space, unoriginated and without beginning, out of which all phenomena arises. The Sanskrit means "the essence of phenomena" and the Tibetan means "the expanse of phenomena" but usually it refers to the emptiness which is the essence of phenomena.

dharmapala (Skt. *dharmapala*, Tib. *chö chong*?) These are beings who are on a higher realm than the human realm who dedicate their life to protecting the dharma. Some protectors were malevolent beings who were converted to protecting the dharma by great trantric practitioners.

dharmatā (Tib. *chö nyi*) Dharmatā is often translated as "suchness" or "the true nature of things" or "things as they are." It is phenomena as it really is or as seen by a completely enlightened being without any distortion or obscuration so one can say it is "reality."

dhyāna meditation (Tib. *sam ten*) The Sanskrit refers to "meditation" but in this context it refers to "mental stability" in relation to śamatha.

disturbing emotions (Skt. kleśa, Tib. *nyön mong*) The emotional obscurations (in contrast to intellectual obscurations) which are also translated as "poisons." The three main disturbing emotions are (passion or desire), (aggression or anger); and (ignorance or delusion). The five disturbing emotions are the three above plus pride andjealousy.

emptiness (Skt. *śūnyatā* Tib. *tong pa nyi*) Also translated as voidness. The Buddha taught in the second turning of the wheel of dharma that external phenomena and the internal phenomena or concept of self or "I" have no real existence and therefore are "empty."

father tantra (Tib. *pha gyu*) There are three kinds of tantras. The father tantra is concerned with transforming aggression, the mother tantra with transforming passion and the non-dual tantra with ignorance.

five wisdoms (Tib. *yeshe nga*) Upon reaching enlightenment, the eight consciousnesses are transformed into the five wisdoms: the mirror-like wisdom, discriminating wisdom, the wisdom of equality, the all-accomplishing wisdom, and the dharmadhatū wisdom.

four noble truths (Tib. *pak pay den pa shi*) The Buddha began teaching with a talk in India at Saranath on the four noble truths. These are the truth of suffering, the truth of the cause of suffering, the cessation of suffering, and the path. These truths are the foundation of Buddhism, particularly the Theravādin path.

four preliminaries (Tib. ngondro and pronounced "nundro") One usually begins the vajrayāna path by doing the four preliminary practices which involve about 100,000 refuge prayers and prostrations, 100,000 vajrasattva mantras,

100,000 maṇḍala offerings, and 100,000 guru yoga practices.

Gampopa (1079-1153 C. E.) One of the main lineage holders of the Kagyu lineage in Tibet. Known also for writing the *Jewel Ornament of Liberation.*

garuḍa (Tib. *khyung*) A mythical bird which hatches fully grown.

kalpa (Tib. *kal pa,* Skt. *yuga*) An eon which lasts in the order of millions of years.

jñāna (Tib. *ye she*) Enlightened wisdom which is beyond dualistic thought.

Indrabodhi (Tib. *rgyal po indra bodhi*) An Indian king during the time of the Buddha who become an accomplished master.

Kagyu (Tib.) One of the four major schools of Buddhism in Tibet. It was founded by Marpa and is headed by His Holiness Karmapa. The other three are the Nyingma, the Sakya, and the Gelupa schools.

karma (Tib. *lay*) Literally "action." Karma is a universal law that when one does a wholesome action one's circumstances will improve and when one does an unwholesome action negative results will eventually occur from the act.

Karmapa The title of 17 sucessive incarnations of Dusum Khyenpa who has headed the Karma Kagyu school of Tibetan Buddhism.

kleśa (Tib. *nyön mong*) The emotional obscurations (in contrast to intellectual obscurations) which are also translated as "poisons." The three main kleśas are (passion or desire or attachment), (aggression or anger); and (ignorance or delusion or aversion). The five kleśas are the three above plus pride and (envy or jealousy).

loving-kindness (Skt. *maitrī,* Tib. *jam pa*) This is compassion for oneself and is a prerequisite to compassion for others (Skt. *karuṇā*).

Madhyamaka (Tib. *u ma*) This is a philosophical school founded by Nāgārjuna in the second century. The main principle of this school is proving that everything is empty of self-nature as usually understood using rational reasoning.

Mahakala ((Tib. *nakpo chenpo*) A chief dharma protector who is the wrathful manifestation of Avalokiteśvara. He is known as the "great black one" and is called Bernakchen.

mahāmudrā (Tib. *cha ja chen po*) Literally means "great seal." As in all phenomena are sealed by the primordiay perfect true nature. Lineage began by Saraha (10th century) is a method of examining mind directly.

mahāyāna (Tib. *tek pa chen po*) Literally, the "great vehicle." These are the teachings of the second turning of the wheel of dharma, which emphasize śūnyatā, compassion, the conduct of a bodhisattva.

Maitreya (Tib. *Jampa*) A bodhisattva at the time of Buddha and is presently residing in Tuṣhita heaven until the coming of the fifth buddha of this kalpa.

maṇḍala (Tib. *chin kor*) A diagram used in various vajrayāna practices, which usually has a central deity and four directions. It also denotes a sacred location such as the maṇḍala of the dharmakāya and this is how it is used in this text.

mantra (Tib. *ngak*) Literally, "protection of the mind" and refers to reciting Sanskrit syllables as part of vajrayāna practice.

mantrayāna Another term for the vajrayāna.

Marpa (1012-1097 C. E.) Marpa was known for being a Tibetan who made three trips to India and brought back many tantric texts including the Six Yogas of Naropa, the Guhyasamāja, and the Chakrasaṃvara practices. His teacher was Tilopa and he founded the Kagyu lineage in Tibet.

meditative absorption (Skt. *samādhi*, Tib. *ting nge dzin*) This is one-pointed meditation and is the highest form of meditation.

Milarepa (1040-1123 C. E.) Milarepa was a student of Marpa who attained enlightenment in one lifetime. His student Gampopa founded the (Dagpo) Kagyu lineage.

mother tantra (Tib. *ma gyu*) There are three kinds of tantras. The father tantra which is concerned with transforming aggression, the mother tantra which concerns transforming passion and the non-dual tantra which concerns ignorance.

nādī (Tib. *tsa*) Subtle channels through which the subtle energies (vayū) flow.

nāga (Tib. *lu*) A water spirit which may take the form of a serpent. It is often the custodian of treasures either texts or actual material treasures under ground.

Nāgārjuna (Tib. *ludrup)* An Indian scholar in the second century who founded the Madhyamaka philosophical school which emphasized emptiness.

Nāropa (956-1040 C. E.) An Indian master who is best known for transmitting many vajrayāna teachings to Marpa who took these back to Tibet before the moslem invasion of India.

ngondro (Tib. and pronounced "nundro") Tibetan for preliminary practice. One usually begins the vajrayāna path by doing the four preliminary practices which involve about 100,000 refuge prayers and prostrations, 100,000 vajrasattva mantras, 100,000 maṇḍala offerings, and 100,000 guru yoga practices.

Padmasambhava (Tib. *Guru Rinpoche*) He was invited to Tibet in the ninth century C. E. and is known for pacifying the nonBuddhist forces and founding the Nyingma lineage.

paṇḍita (Tib. *paṇ ḍi ta*) A great scholar.

pāramitās, six (Tib. *parol tu chinpa*) Sanskrit for "perfections" and the Tibetan literally means "gone to the other side." These are the six practices of the mahāyāna path: Transcendent generosity (dāna), transcendent discipline (śila), transcendent patience (kṣānti), transcendent exertion (virya), transcendent meditation (dhyāna), and transcendent knowledge (prajñā). The ten pāramitās are these plus aspirational prayer, power, and prajñā.

Prajñāpāramitā (Tib. *sherab chi parol tu chin pa*) The Buddhist literature outlining the mahāyāna path and emptiness written mostly around the second century.

prāṇa (Tib. *bindu*) Life supporting energy.

prātimokṣa vows (Tib. *so sor tar pa*) The vows of not killing, stealing, lying, etc. which are taken by monks and nuns.

preliminary practices (Tib. *ngöndro*) The four preliminary practices which are done before doing yidam practice. See ngöndro.

pure realm (Tib. *dag zhing*) Realms created by buddhas which are totally free from suffering and dharma there can be received directly. These realms are presided over by various buddhas such as Amitabha, Avalokiteśvara, and Maitreya who presides over Tuśita.

Ratnasambhava (Tib. *rinchen jungne*) The sambhogakāya buddha of the ratna family.

Śākya Paṇḍita A hereditary head of the Sakya lineage. A great scholar lived 1181-1251 C. E. and was an outspoken opponent of the Kagyu teachings. He also became head of the Tibetan state under the authority of the Mongol emperors.

Śākyamuni Buddha (Tib. *shakya tubpa*) The Śākyamuni Buddha, often called the Gautama Buddha, refers to the latest Buddha who lived between 563 and 483 B. C. E.

samādhi (Tib. *tin ne zin*) Also called meditative absorption or one-pointed meditation, this is the highest form of meditation.

śamatha or tranquility meditation (Tib. *shinay)* This is basic sitting meditation in which one usually follows the breath while observing the workings of the mind while sitting in the crosslegged posture.

samaya (Tib. *dam sig*) The vows or commitments made in the vajrayāna which can be to a teacher or to a practice.

saṃsāra (Tib. *kor wa*) Conditioned existence of ordinary life in which suffering occurs because one still possesses attachment, aggression, and ignorance. It is contrasted to nirvāṇa.

saṅgha (Tib. *gen dun*) These are the companions on the path. They may be all the persons on the path or the noble saṅgha, which are the realized ones.

Śāntideva (675- 725 C. E.) A great bodhisattva who lived in 7th and 8th century in India known for his two works on the conduct of a bodhisattva.

Śāntarakṣita (eighth century C. E.) An abbot of Nālandā University who was invited by King Trisong Detsen to come to Tibet. He established Samye Monastery and thus helped introduce Buddhism in Tibet.

Saraha One of the eighty-four mahāsiddhas of India who was known for his spiritual songs about mahāmudrā.

śāstra (Tib. *tan chö*) The Buddhist teachings are divided into words of the Buddha (the sūtras) and the commentaries of others on his works (the śāstras).

sending and taking practice (Tib. *tong len*) A meditation practice promulgated by Atiśa in which the practitioner takes on the negative conditions of others and gives out all that is positive.

Shentong school (Tib.) The Madhyamika or middle way school divided into two major schools: the Rongtong which maintains voidness is devoid of inherent existence and Shentong which maintains voidness is indivisible from luminosity.

siddha (Tib. *drup top)* An accomplished Buddhist practitioner.

Six Yogas of Nāropa (Tib. *naro chödruk*) These six special yogic practices were transmitted from Nāropa to Marpa and consist of the subtle heat practice, the illusory body practice, the dream yoga practice, the luminosity practice, the ejection of consciousness practice, and the bardo practice.

śrāvaka (Tib. *nyen thö*) Literally "those who hear" meaning disciples. A type of realized hīnayāna practitioner (arhat) who has achieved the realization of the nonexistence of personal self.

stūpa (Tib. *chö ten*) A dome shaped monument to the Buddha which often contains relics and remains of the Buddha or great bodhisattvas.

subtle heat (Tib. *tummo*) An advanced vajrayāna practice for combining bliss and emptiness which produces heat as a byproduct.

śūnyatā (Tib. *tong pa nyi*) Usually translated as voidness or emptiness. The Buddha taught in the second turning of the wheel of dharma that external phenomena and internal phenomena or the concept of self or "I" have no real existence and therefore are "empty."

sūtra (Tib. *do*) These are the hīnayāna and mahāyāna texts which are the words of the Buddha. These are often contrasted with the tantras which are the Buddha's vajrayāna teachings and the śāstras which are commentaries on the words of the Buddha.

sūtrayāna The sūtra approach to achieving enlightenment which includes the hīnayāna and the mahāyāna.

tantra (Tib. *gyu)* The texts of the vajrayāna practices.

Theravādin (Tib. *neten depa*) Specifically a follower of the Sthaviravada school of the hīnayāna. Here refers to the first teachings of the Buddha which emphasized the careful examination of mind and its confusion.

three jewels (Tib. *kön chok sum*) These are the Buddha, the dharma, and the saṅgha.

Tilopa (928-1009 C. E.) One of the eighty-four mahāsiddhas who became the guru of Nāropa who transmitted his teachings to the Kagyu lineage in Tibet.

torma (Tib., Skt. *bali*) A ritual object made of dried barley and butter and put on the shrine used as a symbolic offering to the dieties.

tradition of profound view (Tib. *ta wa zap mo*)This tradition is one of the principal mahayana traditions in India which was founded by Nagarjuna in the 2nd century C. E. It is the Madhyamaka "middle way" that teaches emptiness of all external and internal phenomena.

tradition of vast conduct (Tib. *chö pa gya chen po*) This tradition is one of the two principal mahāyāna traditions in India founded by Asangha in the fourth century C. E. It is the Cittamātra or "mind only" school that teaches how all phenomena are mind created. It gave rise to the mahāyāna traditions of Abhidharma and logic.

ultimate truth (Tib. *dondam*) This ultimate truth which can only be perceived by an enlightened individual is that all phenomena both internal (thoughts and feelings) and external (the outside physical world) does not have any inherent existence.

vajra (Tib. *dorje*) Usually translated "diamond like." This may be an implement held in the hand during certain vajrayāna ceremonies, or it can refer to a quality which is so pure and so enduring that it is like a diamond.

Vajrapāṇi (Tib. *Channa Dorje*) A major bodhisattva said to be lord of the mantra and a major protector of Tibetan Buddhism.

Vajrayoginī (Tib. *Dorje Palmo*) A semiwrathful yidam.

vajrayāna (Tib. *dorje tek pa*) There are three major traditions of Buddhism (hīnayāna, mahāyāna, vajrayāna) The vajrayāna is based on the tantras and emphasizes the clarity aspect of phenomena and is mainly practiced in Tibet.

Vinaya (Tib. *dul wa*) These are the teachings by the Buddha concerning proper conduct. There are seven main precepts that may be observed by lay persons and 125 or 320 to be observed by monks and nuns.

vipaśyanā meditation (Tib. *lha tong*) Sanskrit for "insight meditation" This meditation develops insight into the nature of mind. The other main meditation is śamatha meditation.

wish-fulfilling jewel (Tib. *yid shin norbu*) A jewel said to exist in the naga or deva realms which gave the owner whatever he or she wanted. Now used mostly metaphorically.

yāna (Tib. *thek pa*) Literally means vehicle but refers here to level of teaching. There are three main yānas (see hīnayāna, mahāyāna, and vajrayāna).

yidam (Skt. *iṣṭadevatā*) A trantric deity that embodies qualities of Buddhahood and is practiced in the vajrayāna. Also called a tutelary deity.

yogatantra (Tib. *naljor gyi gyu*) Literally, "union tantra" and refers to a tantra that places emphasis on internal meditations.

Glossary of Tibetan Terms

Pronounced	Spelled	English
bag yod pa	bag yod pa	alertness
barma rabjung	bar me rab byang	ordin.ordination
brtson 'grus	brtson 'grus	diligence
bsam gtan	bsam gtan	5th paramita
bsam pa	bsam pa	contemplating
cha ja chen po	phyag rgya chen po	māmudrā
chang chup chi sem	byang chub kyi sems	bodhicitta
chang chup sem pa	byang chub sems 'dpa	bodhisattva
che rim	bskyed rim	generation stage
chö	chos	dharma
chö ngön pa	chos mngon pa	Abhidharma
chö ying	chos dbyings	dharmadhātu
chogo	chos gos	yellow robe
chö ying	chos dbyings	dharmadhatu
dam tsig	dam tsig	samaya vow
de no sum	sde snod gsum	Tripitaka
ding ba	gding ba	seat clothing
dom pa	sdomg pa	vows
do de	mdo sde	sūtras
dom sum	sdomg sum	three vows
don yod grub pa	don yod grub pa	amaghassiddhi
dren pa	dren pa	mindfulness
dul ba	'dul ba	vinaya
du tim	dus khrims	temporary
dzo rim	rdzogs rim	completion stage
gagye	dgag dbye	relaxed period
gelong	dge slong	bhikṣhu
gelongma	dge slong ma	bhikṣhuni
genyen	dge bsnyen	genyan vow
getsul	dge tsul	intermediate ord.

gom	sgom	meditation
Jampa	byams pa	Maitreya
je thop	rjes thop	post
Kagyu	bka' brgyud	Kagyu school
kal pa	bskal pa	kalpa
khom	goms	habitual tend.
khyung	khyung	garuḍa
korlo dompa	'khor lo sdom pa	Cakrasaṃvara
lay	las	karma
lhag ma	lhag ma	13 reminders
lhag tong	lhag mthog	vipasyana
lo jong	blos byong	mind training
lu	klu	nāga
ludrup	klu sgrub	Nāgārjuna
ma rigpa	ma rig pa	ignorance
mchid	mchid	speech
melong lti iu' yeshe	me long lti iu' ye shes	mirror-like wisdom
michöpa	mi bskyod pa	Akṣobhya
nakpo chenpo	nag po chen po	Mahakala
ngak	sngags	mantra
ngondro	sngon 'gro	prelim. practice
ngo pa	mngon pa	Abhidharma
nyen ne	bsnyen gnas	temporary vow
nyön mong	nyon mongs	kleśa
öpame	'od dpag med	Amitabha
pak pay den pa shi	phags pa'i bden pa bzhi	4 noble truths
pam pa	'pham pa	four defeats
pong tung	spong ltung	30 transgressions
Rinchen Jangden	rin chen'byung ldan	Ratnasambhava
nal jor jyi gyu	rnal 'byor kyi rgyud	yoga tantra
nam par nang dze	rnam par snang mdzad	Vairocana
sa	sa	bodhisattva level
sam pa	bsam pa	meditating
sam ten	bsam gtan	dhyāna meditation
sang ba	sang ba	essential element

sang lam	gsang lam	quick road
sang	gsang	secret
sangye	sangs rgyas	buddha
sbyin pa	sbyin pa	generosity 1st para
sem	sems	mind
sham thab	sham thabs	lower garmet
shar drol	shar grol	lib of illusions
she rab	shes rab	prajna
she zin	shes bzhin pa	awareness
shinye	zhi gnas	shamatha
so sor tharpa	so sor tharpa	individ.liberation
sod pa	rtsod pa	debate
som pa	rtsom pa	composition
sojong	gso sbyong	bimonthly purific.
Songtsen Gampo	srong btsan sgom po	Songtsen Gampo
sor sor tharpa dompa	so sor thar pa'i sdom pa	individual liberat.
spyod pa	spyod pa	action
sumten dorje dzinpa	gsum rten rdo rje dzin pa	holder of 3 vows
ta ba	lta ba	view
tan chö	bstan bcos	commentary
tek pa chen po	theg pa chen po	mahāyāna
ten tim	gtan khrims	permanent
thamal gyi shepa		ordinary mind
thig le	thig le	subtle drops
thos pa	thos pa	hearing
ti mug	gti mug	ignorance
tiglee	thig le	subtle drops
tonglen	glong len	sending & taking
tong pa nyi	strong pa nyid	emptiness
tsa	rtsa	nādī
tsod pa	rtsod pa	debate
tsun pa	btsun pa	well disciplined
tsultrim	tshul khrims	discipline
tsom pa	btsun pa	composition
tummo	gtum mo	subtle heat

u ma	dbu ma	Madhyamaka
yarne	dbyar gbas	rainy retreat
yeshe	ye shes	jñāna
zang po	bzang po	compassionate
zod pa	bzod pa	patience

Bibliography

The Jātaka by the Buddha.

These are stories of the Buddha's previous lives as animals and as people. These tales are part of the Sūtras and the entire Pali editions of these tales have been reprinted by the Pali Text Society in 1957 in six volumes.

Jewel Ornament of Liberation by Gampopa.

This work was originally translated by Herbert Guenther and published by Shambala Publications (Boston) in 1971. There is a newer and in many ways much clearer translation by Ken and Katia Holmes as *Jems of Dharma: Jewels of Fredom* (London: Altea Publications, 1995).

The Mahāmudrā: Eliminating the Darkness of Ignorance by Wangchug Dorje, The Ninth Karmapa (1556-1603).

This text on Mahamudra has been translated by Alexander Berzin Dharamsala, India: Library of Tibetan Works and Archives. 1978.

The Moonlight of Mahamudra by Tashi Namgyal.

This text on mahamudra has been translated by Lobsang Lhalungpa as *Mahamudra: The Quintessence of Mind and Meditation*. Published by Shambhala (Boston) in 1986. Thrangu Rinpoche has done extensive commentaries on this book in his five volume series entitles *The Moonlight of Mahamudra* (Boulder: Namo Buddha Publications)

The King of Samādhi by the Buddha. (Skt. *Samādhi raja sūtra)*

This is one of the few teachings of the Buddha that

discusses mahāmudrā meditation. The first four chapters of this sūtra has been translated by John Rockwell at Naropa Institute and the eleventh chapter was translated by Mark Tatz in his Ph.D. thesis at the University of Washington. Thrangu Rinpoche has given an extensive commentary on this sūtra in the *King of Samādhi*. Boudhanath, Nepal: Rangjung Yeshe Publications, 1994.

The Vinaya by the Buddha

This is one of the three major divisions of the Buddhist teachings which covers the discipline. The Pali versions has been translated by I. B. Horner for the Pali Text Society from 1938 to 1966 in six volumes. The collected the Vinaya and placed it in the Kanjur but this has not at this time been translated into English.

Khenchen Thrangu, Rinpoche

Thrangu Rinpoche was born in Kham in 1933. At the age of four he was formally recognized by the Gyalwa Karmapa and Palpung Situ Rinpoche as the ninth incarnation of the great Thrangu Tulku.

From the age of seven until sixteen he learned to read and write, memorized texts and studied spiritual practices. He then began his formal studies in Buddhist philosophy, psychology, logic, debate, and the Buddhist scriptures with Lama Khenpo Lodro Rabsel. At the age of twenty-three along with Garwang Rinpoche and Chögyam Trungpa Rinpoche, he received the Gelong ordination from the Gyalwa Karmapa. Following this Thrangu Rinpoche engaged in a period of intense practice and received further instructions from his lama, Khenpo Gyangasha Wangpo.

During the Chinese takeover of Tibet when Rinpoche was twenty-seven he left Tibet and was called to Rumtek the seat of the Kagyu lineage in exile. At the time there was great concern that the teachings of the Kagyu lineage, that of, Tilopa, Naropa, Gampopa, Marpa, Milarepa and others would be completely lost. His Holiness Karmapa asked Thrangu Rinpoche to receive teachings from the Tibetan religious scholars and to become one of the first Kagyu lamas to receive a geshe degree. At the age of 35 he earned the degree of Geshe Rabjam from the Dalai Lama and was appointed "Vice Chancellor of the Principle Seat of the Kagyu Vajra Upholder of the Three Disciplines" by His Holiness Karmapa.

Thrangu Rinpoche then returned to Rumtek and became a full holder and teacher of all the Kagyu vajrayana lineages and has a special, direct transmission of the Shentong philosophical tradition. Being so gifted he was chosen to establish the Nalanda Institute of Higher Learning and to teach the Kagyu tulkus. He has also been the personal teacher of the four principal Karma Kagyu tulkus: Shamar Rinpoche, Situ Rinpoche, Gyaltsab Rinpoche, and the late Jamgon Kongtrul Rinpoche.

After teaching at Rumtek for over two dozen years, Thrangu Rinpoche traveled to the West in 1979 and began teaching Western students at Samye Ling monastery in Scotland the teachings he had taught in monastic college. He also established a monastery, a primary school, and an abbey for women practitioners in Kathmandu, Nepal. At Namo Buddha, a famous sacred place visited by Buddha in a previous lifetime, about 20 miles from Kathmandu Thrangu Rinpoche has established a three-year retreat center and monastic college as well as a medical clinic.

Thrangu Rinpoche has since traveled extensively in Europe, North and South America, and the Far East. He is known as a gifted teacher who can take complex teachings and make them accessible to students. He offers a number of yearly Namo Buddha Seminars in Nepal, Europe, and North America for beginning and advanced students of Buddhism. He has also published extensively including *Tranquillity and Insight*, *Buddha Nature*, *King of Samadhi* and a series of books on Mahamudra meditation.

Anyone wishing information about Thrangu Rinpoche's activities, seminars, and publications can contact: Clark Johnson, Ph. D., Namo Buddha Seminar, 1390 Kalmia Avenue, Boulder, CO 80304-1813 or phone (303) 449-6608.